SOUL TALKS

52-Weeks of Inspiration

TALISHA A. MATHESON

Carla,

Happy Reading.

Be Inspired!

Talisha

2021

To my Grandfather, affectionately known as "C.P.,"
You are a man who speaks words filled with truth, humility,
authenticity and wisdom, and for that, I am grateful.

Love you, Grandad

*"You may not control all the events
that happen to you, but you can decide
not to be reduced by them."*

– Maya Angelou

Table of Contents

Dear Reader,..1

Introduction..3

Week One: Be Still Or Be Distracted....................................5

Week Two: Self-Sabotage: When Enough Is Enough..........8

Week Three: Let Your Intuition Speak.............................. 11

Week Four: Expecting You From Others 14

Week Five: I Am Not Impressed.. 17

Week Six: The Battle Is You vs You 19

Week Seven: Friendship Goals! 21

Week Eight: Purge, Emerge & Flourish............................ 24

Week Nine: Let's Get Intimate! 26

Week Ten: Are You Misunderstood?.................................. 29

Week Eleven: Decluttering The Chaos 32

Week Twelve: Emotional Baggage Check 35

Week Thirteen: Extension Of Grace 38

Week Fourteen: Do You Know Your Worth?.................... 40

Week Fifteen: Open Up And Bloom 43

Week Sixteen: Sunshine State Of Mind............................ 46

Week Seventeen: Ultimate Quest To Wholeness 48

Week Eighteen: Stop Faking It! 51

Week Nineteen: Who Pours Into You?.............................. 54

Week Twenty: The Plight Of The Strong Black Woman .. 56

Week Twenty-one: Chit-Chat & All That! 58

Week Twenty-two: Authenticity & Approval 61

Week Twenty-three: It's Time To Break Free 63

Week Twenty-four: How True Are Their Colours?........... 65

Week Twenty-five: A New Perspective.............................. 67

Week Twenty-six: Just Breathe.. 70

Week Twenty-seven: Soul Recognition 72

Week Twenty-eight: Discovering An Ongoing Freedom.. 75

Week Twenty-nine: Love & Appreciation 78

Week Thirty: Do You Have The Capacity To Love? 81
Week Thirty-one: Awakening A Stagnant Mindset 84
Week Thirty-two: Visiting The Past 87
Week Thirty-three: Please Read The Label 90
Week Thirty-four: Start Expecting 93
Week Thirty-five: Move In Love & Forgiveness 95
Week Thirty-six: The Responsibility Is Yours 98
Week Thirty-seven: In The Midst Of Fear 101
Week Thirty-eight: Speak Life! 103
Week Thirty-nine: Insecure, Sure & Unsure 106
Week Forty: From Misery To Joy 109
Week Forty-one: For Love's Sake: Part One 112
Week Forty-two: For Love's Sake: Part Two 115
Week Forty-three: Breaking Down The Walls 118
Week Forty-four: Privacy & Oversharing 120
Week Forty-five: Lost & Found 123
Week Forty-six: Vulnerability: Part One 126
Week Forty-seven: Vulnerability: Part Two 129
Week Forty-eight: The Purpose Of The Struggle 132
Week Forty-nine: A Reason, Season or Lifetime 135
Week Fifty: Understanding Our Needs vs Our Wants 137
Week Fifty-one: Living Life on Purpose 140
Week Fifty-two: Soul Talks 142
Acknowledgements 145
About the Author 146

Dear Reader,

There are days where I write because I have something stirring in my mind that needs to come out. There are also days I need to write because something is imprinted on my soul and requires release.

The words you are about to read on the following pages are pieces of my soul, and I hope, no, I pray they bless you as you receive them, as much as I was blessed writing them.

You see, words set my soul on fire, and *Soul Talks: 52-Weeks of Inspiration* is not just another book. It's an inspirational journey curated from a place of pain to healing.

It's an intimate conversation with your past, present and future self that will encourage you to ask tough questions of others and turn those questions inwards and apply, reflect and answer them as a means to shift from pain to peace, healing and growth.

I believe in the spectacular power that words possess, and this collection of internal musings and never-ending questions has brought me to realizations I never thought possible.

I invite you to kick off your shoes, open your mind and relax and join me as we feel all the feelings and have a chuckle or two along the way. I am not an expert by any means, nor do I have all the answers, but I believe in the influence of conversation and reflection and that speaking our way through our experiences will allow us to move forward.

Soul Talks is vulnerability, authenticity, enlightenment and transparency between the lines so, let's live, love and laugh ourselves to a destination we once thought was unreachable.

Be Inspired!
Talisha

"A safe space is any space that feels nurturing and allows your feelings to be what they are."

– Christine Einge

Introduction

Before we get into the nitty-gritty of things over the next fifty-two weeks, I wanted to make you aware of a term you will see over and over again, and I thought it would be a good idea to put it into context as a foundation of sorts.

To be safe is to be protected from something or someone. It's a state of not being exposed to danger or risk, and it's the act of avoiding harm or loss.

I didn't understand the importance of an emotionally safe space until I started to pay attention to my emotions and how I felt before, during and after spending time with different groups of people and one on one with specific individuals. I realized the places I expected to be safe were not, and I had to come to terms with that revelation.

An emotionally safe space is where you can unload without hesitation. It's a place that is judgement-free, one where you will not be criticized, blamed, rejected, invalidated or dismissed. It's a space where you don't have the desire to defend yourself or your feelings. It's a place where you are seen and heard even if you're not fully understood. Your feelings matter not in theory but actuality.

Let's dig deeper. A safe space is where the other person or persons actively listen rather than push their point of view on a matter. It's a space where when you leave, you are sure the vault closes behind you, and your "stuff" is contained in that person's safety.

For me, a safe space must include trust, honesty, vulnerability and empathy. The formula may be different for each of you, but the most important thing is that you have one. Also, recognize that just because we are a safe space for someone doesn't mean that person is our safe space. Unfortunately, many of us unknowingly make this emotionally destructive mistake but rest assured it can be rectified.

I also recently discovered something that gave me additional pause. I need to be a safe space for myself and have the ability to work through things independently while having a safe emotional space with others. Both spaces are critical to healing and growth because they need to be a place where I can lean in and be my whole self and have rest, comfort and peace.

And with that, I want to ask a few questions. Are you a safe space for yourself? Do you have a safe space with others? Who are they? How do they make you feel, and why? Are you a safe space for others?

"Finding a human that you can be vulnerable with while feeling completely safe is priceless."

– j.iron word

If you have a safe space, I am happy for you. If you are unsure about your space, I hope the above questions and weeks of emotional digging will help give you clarity, and if you don't have a safe space yet, I want you to know that you will find one once your formula is determined.

So, here's to us setting the tone for the coming weeks, understanding the importance of emotional safety, and seeking our safe spaces, one day, one week, and one page at a time.

Be Inspired!

Week
One

Be Still Or Be Distracted

"Be still and know that I am God..."

— *Psalms 46:10 KJV*

A short verse from the Bible inspired my theme for 2020 and 2021. It was to the point that I had to post it on my fridge as a daily reminder.

At the beginning of 2020, I didn't understand how that verse aligned with my life or what it was supposed to mean to me, but I was open to seeing where it would lead. Little did I know it would direct me to a place of physical and mental stillness and surrender.

As the year progressed, I began to understand the importance of stillness and why it was a necessary focus for me during this season of my life. It forced me to face some demons I thought I conquered. It pushed me to open my mind, despite thinking it was already open. It was a time of revelation and surprise, and I wouldn't have experienced it without being still.

When the year ended, I felt rejuvenated and expected the new year to present a new word and a new focus, but stillness continued to be on the tip of my tongue, and now I understand why. My lesson from 2020 wasn't over.

Some of us have a noise of choice where we consume ourselves with what other people are doing or not doing. Saying or not saying and acting or not acting and don't realize it's a form of distraction. First, it's none of our business what others are doing, and it's just plain nosey and second, what we are primarily doing is deflecting from the things we need to work on individually.

I am trying to understand why we prefer distraction over dealing with the things that will eventually catapult us into a higher dimension of living and loving. Why are we deliberately choosing distraction over stillness? What has us so afraid to face ourselves?

Perhaps we choose noise over silence and stillness because the noise distracts us from the things that need to be corrected. Noise shifts our focus and blurs the finite details of where we and our lives require improvement. It stops us from having that difficult conversation with a loved one or making a decision we have been flip-flopping on for a while. It prevents us from telling someone how we genuinely feel or making the necessary changes to make our lives better. To make us better.

As quickly as we embrace the noise as a tactic to deter and avoid, perhaps we need to have the same quickness to starve the distraction and stop it dead in its tracks. We can only ignore situations for so long before they morph into a tsunami, destroying everything in its path.

I believe distractions keep us in a never-ending cycle of worry and disappointment. However, when we encounter the sweetness of being still, it prepares us for a journey of beauty, revelation and endless opportunity.

A friend asked me what it meant to me to be still, and for once, I didn't have to mull it over because the words had been stirring in me for months. I don't know if I did it justice when asked, so I hope to do it now.

To me, being still is like driving down that long road on any day and permitting myself to look to the left and the right to absorb my surroundings. It's stopping to let the sun beat down on my face and feel a smile creep across my lips. Being still is feeling something bubble in my soul and not shy away from it, but allow myself to experience its warmth and acknowledge that it's joy without borders.

I think amid the stillness, we find growth. I consider it to be an incubation period where we can all feel safe.

Being still is taking the time to think before we speak and react and allow ourselves to use all of our senses and permit ourselves to feel all the feelings. Being still gives us the freedom to sit in our feelings for as long as we want.

I want to challenge you to starve your distractions and feed the idea of embracing stillness, knowing it will take you to places you never thought possible.

Be Inspired!

Week
Two

Self-Sabotage:
When Enough Is Enough

---

*"Self-sabotage is when we say
we want something and then go about
making sure it doesn't happen."*

— *Alyce Cornyn-Selby*

I have the gift of talking myself out of things regularly. I can justify buying the same pair of boots in all available colours because they are pretty and comfortable. But I possess an identical dedication when talking myself out of doing things that are good for me. I used to think it was out of pure stubbornness, but I have realized it was a lack of belief in myself and my capabilities.

Have you ever talked yourself out of something you know is good for you only to convince yourself that a dead end is the better choice? I know it doesn't sound brilliant, but it's how we speak to ourselves and move through our lives.

I often wonder if self-sabotage is born from a fear of failure, or perhaps it's ignited by a fear of succeeding and the responsibility that coincides with success. It could come from a lack of self-confidence. Maybe it's easier to identify self-sabotage when we stand in the place of a bystander rather than a participant.

As a bystander, we notice an individual always finds a reason why something won't work. We will also come in contact with the person who consistently complains yet never wants a solution to their struggle. Whatever the sabotage mechanism and no matter what position we are in as saboteurs or bystanders, none of the above results in progress in any way, shape or form. Self-sabotage is like furiously moving in quicksand. The more you flail in panic, the deeper you sink, and we end up stuck.

More often than not, we allow opportunities to approach us, slap us in the face and walk away, then have the audacity to question why we are not progressing.

But why are we so willing to sabotage without hesitation? Why do we openly embrace the things that will end in demise but turn our backs on the good? Why are we so comfortable being the roadblock in our lives?

I would hate to think we have found comfort in our dysfunction and feel that we don't deserve peace and happiness. Could we possibly not believe in our skills and abilities or think we don't deserve better? And as sad as it sounds, I think that might be the very reason.

Sometimes we get so used to fighting to the point of exhaustion that the thought of a smooth life scares the crap out of us. We sit in angst, biting our nails and looking over our shoulders, anticipating the doom and gloom, never enjoying the moment. Why has peace, calm and happiness become foreign?

I talked to a member of my tribe, and we had a good laugh on this very topic. We were saying that when things go smoothly, that is when we hold our breath the longest. As if we are bracing ourselves for the inevitable crap to hit the fan. We embrace chaos and turmoil with open arms, only to emerge feeling like an emotional wreck and somehow believe we have won.

We then agreed that we miss out on joy while holding our breath, closing our eyes, and fighting!

I want us all to bring the normalcy back to celebrating when things go well, no matter how small. I want us to stop holding our breath when the ship of life is sailing and lean back and enjoy the ride. I want us to stop making excuses as to why we can't do something. I want us to stop looking over our shoulders for something terrible to happen and remain focused on the goodness coming our way. I want us to enjoy the moments, take risks and breath through our inevitable fear. But most of all, I want us to get out of our way.

Be Inspired!

Week Three

Let Your Intuition Speak

"Never apologize for trusting your intuition – your brain can play tricks, your heart can be blind, but your gut is always right."

— *Rachel Wolchin*

First and foremost, I would like to offer an extended apology to my intuition for all of the gut feelings I have ignored over the years. To all of the nudges and unsettled feelings that were telling me something wasn't right. I am sincerely sorry for not considering you when I made decisions without consulting you first.

I know many of us pride ourselves on our intuition, and if any of you are like me, you tend to get a gut feeling about certain things and people. Also, if you are like me, you may ignore that gut feeling and chalk it up to overthinking or even go as far as to label it as paranoia. But let me clarify that intuition is natural, and if your gut tells you something isn't right, it's not right.

When my paternal grandmother would meet someone, she would say in her soft Grenadian accent that "her spirit doesn't take her or him," and to give you a North American translation, she was simply saying that "there is something about this person I don't like." You see, she was always in tune with people and situations and what we saw as stubbornness; in hindsight, I understand now that she was connected to her intuition.

I think about many situations where I listened to my gut and ended up on top and avoided disasters. Then I think of other times where my gut was on a loudspeaker, telling me to flee. Yet, I decided to walk into the eye of the storm only to realize I could have avoided the pain had I had listened to who I now proudly call my inner self.

I think we all have her or him dwelling inside us, but the problem is discerning intuition versus overthinking. I believe our intuition is steady, unwavering and rational. On the other hand, overthinking is unrealistic if we are honest and shifts as often as our moods.

We look at intuition and paranoia as synonyms, and they are not. So I want us to create a special space for our intuition because it's that important. It resides somewhere that other feelings can't compete. We need to lean in and listen to our intuition and make it as normal as texting or calling a friend for advice. Making intuition our friend can save us from many heartaches provided we pay closer attention to it.

I think back, and I could have saved myself from years of rollercoasters and one hundred or so grey hairs if only I had paid closer attention and didn't write off my intuition as me being cynical.

Time for perspective:

By ignoring the nudges, we feel we are deliberately not trusting ourselves.

Let's learn to trust our gut and realize it's not indigestion but our inner brain telling us something isn't right. And let me clarify something as well, our gut instinct isn't just for adverse situations. It also tells us when something is ok.

We tend to think trusting our gut only exists when we are trying to avoid disaster, but it also exists when we are about to walk into something that will change the trajectory of our lives for the better.

So do yourself a favour and reintroduce yourself to your intuition. Apologize, reconnect and make her or him part of your life again. You can thank me later.

Be Inspired!

Week Four

Expecting You From Others

"The biggest disappointment is expecting YOU from other people."

— *Unknown*

There comes a time when we become self-aware and stop expecting people to speak how we want them to speak and listen when we want them to listen and react in a way we deem appropriate. We will also understand that when we expect these things, we are interfering with people's individuality. The moment we expect someone's response to align with our ideas is when we attempt to strip them of their individuality.

You see, we tend to expect reactions to situations to match how we think they "should" be, but we need to remember we are not writing a script for a character in a movie. We are dealing with real life, real situations, real emotions and real people.

I have an ongoing conversation with people who are dissatisfied with their love relationships. The common thread is that there is a consistent sense of their partner not loving them in a way they deem acceptable, for lack of a better word. Because of this, I want us to assess our relationships and then dig in and find out why the dissatisfaction exists.

We have all endured moments of dissatisfaction in our relationships, but I will step on the other side of this and make a bold statement that will make some uncomfortable. We want our mates to love us based on our expectations, not their capabilities, and this is where disappointment lives. We sometimes want them to love us how we would love, not how they are capable of loving. It's like getting a left-handed individual to use their right hand and expect them to complete tasks without difficulty or error.

How much of our dissatisfaction would exist if we gave our mates the height, depth and breadth to love us in their way?

Don't get me wrong, love languages are an essential block in the foundation of our relationships, and we need to pay attention to them, but what if there was more to it? What if we gave our mates the freedom to love the way they want in conjunction with how we need to be loved? And what if we stopped limiting the kind of love we are willing to receive and open ourselves to a broader range of loving?

Let me paint a picture for you. My top love languages are Physical Touch and Quality time. Suppose my mate was to love me in my love language plus his love language. By adding say Words of Affirmation and Acts of Service, I end up receiving love beyond what I expect and in ways that I never knew I needed, and if I do the same, we are both satisfied on levels beyond our expectations.

We all came from different spaces and lived experiences that shape how we operate and react in various circumstances. And yes, there is always room for adjustment, learning and improvement, but first, we need to offer the people in our lives the appropriate space to do it their way.

Essentially we need to stop expecting ourselves from other people. Stop expecting people to love as we love, give as we give and do as we do. Why? Because they are not you or me! Doing so will save us a lot of confusion, disappointment and heartache in our relationship circles.

I also wonder, could our relationship dissatisfaction brew from a lack of open and careful communication? Perhaps we fail to communicate what we need, and as a result, have unrealistic expectations that our mate is supposed to read our minds. We can't rely on telepathy to aid in the success of our relationships.

What if we had more conversations about the state of our relationships with our partners? Doing so doesn't remove the romance; I would think it enhances what is already there because now your partner can see that you are committed to loving them wholly and correctly. And don't we all desire to be loved correctly?

Love shows its face differently and without a specific look or feel. Perhaps we need to adjust our pre-conceived notion of how things "should" be and take a step back. Let's remove the chains on love, mates, and relationships and discover love freely without a script. We might be surprised by what transpires.

Be Inspired!

Week Five

I Am Not Impressed

---

*"I don't believe in titles;
they make people feel superior."*

— Henry Ford

I am always intrigued when I ask someone how they are, and instead of answering the question, they find a way to throw in all of the titles they carry. I mean, no one asked for a resume; I literally want to know how they are.

It makes me smile and then frown because it's clear that many people are so attached to their job titles that they can't separate who they are from what they do. There is a difference!

Money and titles don't impress me, nor do they drive me to do more or be more. And when I say these things, people naturally look at me sideways and think I am just honourable, but as God, as my witness, I am truthful when I say the title and the dollar signs that coincide with them do not drive me.

I have seen what that type of drive can do to a person in both body and mind and personality, for that matter, and I want nothing to do with it. The reason I say this is because as quickly as promotion happens, demotion is right around the corner, and as swiftly as pay increases are signed, the demand for your time, energy and bits of your soul is lurking beyond the dotted line.

I am not saying I lack ambition or desire to work for free because we need ambition and money, but we also need to look inside ourselves and identify why we do what we do. If the reason is solely for a high salary, fame, status, or anything superficial, maybe it's for the wrong reasons.

Is there passion and fulfillment in what you do? Would you do it for free? Those are the questions I had asked myself when I was chasing position and money, and the answer was a resounding no. And I thank God for keeping so many of those doors closed because I soon realized that what I thought I wanted to do no longer existed. The things I set aside because they "didn't" or "couldn't" pay as well became the very thing that gives me joy, fulfillment and an overall sense of purpose and happiness. Funny how life can throw you a curveball.

And right when you think you have it all figured out, you realize you have been walking down the wrong path for a while. Thankfully there is always a way to get to the other side via the ominous fork in the road, which will bring us back to where we need to be.

Find the thing that feeds your soul and do it. You won't regret it.

Be Inspired!

Week
Six

The Battle Is You vs You

---

*"Talk to yourself like you would
to someone you love."*

— Brené Brown

Quick question for you, would you let anyone talk to you the way you speak to yourself? Yup, we are jumping right in on this one—no gentle introduction, just a hard and fast question to get your emotional wheels in motion.

Maybe it's just me, but I have some very disrespectful conversations with myself some days. The things I say, I would never allow another human to speak to me in the same manner. NEVER!

First, I would ask them who they thought they are talking to and request a change in their tone before continuing. Then I would go into my sassy archive and question where this person mustered up the audacity. You see, all of this is good and well in theory, except I never ask these things of myself. I never stand up for myself to myself. Have you?

Have you ever stopped yourself from breaking down the very fabric of your being? Have you ever told yourself to stop and have more respect for your reflection? Have you ever refrained from pouring salt into your open wounds? Have you given yourself grace? I ask you these questions because I wonder why we hesitate when it's time to stand in our corner?

As much as we love and appreciate ourselves, provided we do, of course. I think there are times when we forget who we are. It's the portion of ourselves that allows the mindset of yesteryear to creep into our present state, causing us to forget how hard we worked to be where we are. It's the part of us that fails to see where we belong.

We all have a natural desire to have others speak well of us and be kind because it's the humane and decent thing to do. But I wonder. How can we demand and expect that treatment from others when we fail to do so for ourselves? It's is a tough question to ask and an even tougher pill to swallow, but it is necessary.

I think gentle and constructive conversations with ourself is required for us to heal, not just from the abuse and trauma caused by others, but the abuse and trauma caused by our negative self-talk. The latter is a place where we need to take full responsibility. Do you agree?

I want to give you a challenge this week. Each time you have a negative thought directed inwards or say it aloud at your reflection, I want you to practice following it up with something positive. Why? Because I want you to clean up your language in the moment. I want you to adjust your tone and speak love, life and healing to the person who is consistently and will be eternally by your side. You!

Be Inspired!

Friendship Goals!

"Friends are the family you choose."

— Jess C. Scott

I have been thinking about friendships lately and how important it is to have a solid group of people who roll with you through the ebbs and flows of life. I have also pondered how freely we use the word "friend," and I have been challenging myself for years to be careful with whom I give the honourable title.

The reason is that not everyone you converse with or spend time with is your friend. Not everyone in your life is FOR you, and the sooner we recognize that, the less complicated our circles will be and the more quality people we will have to enrich our lives.

You may ask what it means to have someone FOR you, so let me break it down. The people who are FOR you are the ones who recognize your silence as pain, frustration, contemplation or worry. They don't tell you;

you're moody, miserable, absent or uncommunicative. They hear your silence loud and clear and can translate it into the words you cannot speak.

We know people come into our lives for a reason, a season and a lifetime. For me, some were there to teach me a lesson and allow for growth, while others were short-lived and faded without another thought.

Then my lifetime people, well, we're still on the journey. I especially embrace the ones who have come full circle. We lost touch as we fumbled through our twenties and thirties, and BAM! we're back as if no time has passed.

I am blessed to have a solid group of people in my friend circle, both male and female, because I like balance. They consist of individuals who support me, call me out when I'm wrong, and some of them have the uncanny knack of translating my silence.

They are my comrades, my tribe, my kin. They allow me to live and be my authentic self. They make me laugh, most times at the dumbest things, and I love each of them. I couldn't ask for a more fantastic group of individuals to be part of my life.

We have rallied around each other, chastised one another, laughed until we cried and cried until we laughed. We have prayed, sang songs and fought over the lyrics and enjoyed every moment in between.

"Normalize using words such as colleague, classmate, acquaintance, old school mate, neighbour and client. Not everyone is your friend."

— *Unknown*

Have you frivolously used the word friend? Do you give the title to anyone, or do you hold it closely like a treasured gem?

I ask because we tend to forget that mutual social media followers are strangers and not friends. Sometimes the people you work with are just colleagues, and there is nothing wrong with that, so I hope we get into the habit of using the word with caution. I hope you have a solid group of people as I do. Call them what you like: your tribe, your people, your crew. No matter the name, ensure they know how much they mean to you. Love them, hug them, appreciate them and keep them close.

Be Inspired!

Week Eight

Purge, Emerge & Flourish

"Purge, emerge and flourish.
It's a natural thing to do."

— *Unknown*

I am in a self-induced season of purging. It's a purge of my physical space as well as my relationship space. I am honest with myself more than usual during this time, restricting my capacity to embrace anything that will not assist in growth. I am deliberate in limiting who has access to me in my physical space and my mental space.

This year the purge affected me differently, and I give credit to this new version of myself. I am not limiting the purge to the tangible. I am extending it to the people in my life, ensuring it's not coming from a place of malice or dislike towards them, but from a place of love and respect for myself and recognizing that I matter.

I have said it before, and maybe we all need to be reminded that just because someone is in your life for a period doesn't mean they are FOR you.

Having a DNA connection or a formal title in your life is not a prerequisite for gaining complete access to you, and perhaps the moment we accept that will be the moment things begin to shift.

It's no secret I like to shop. And not just when I am happy, I like to shop amid all emotions, including just because the sun is shining. And as hard as it may be to believe, as much as I find satisfaction in acquiring nice things, I find it equally satisfying to go through my space and remove any clutter. It's such a rush!

You see, this season of purging includes a new mentality. No longer am I holding on to things with a "just in case" mindset. You know what I mean. It's that item you keep pushing to the back of your closet or bottom drawer. Purge after purge only to realize it's been ten years, and you have yet to wear it.

I mention this because we go through the same process with some people in our lives as we do with clothing. What is the point of holding on to the remnants of friendships and past relationships? Is it just to say we have them? What is the point of wearing our pain like a badge of honour when it's really a noose separating us from accessible joy?

Let's take a step back and recognize that past hurt and pain are there for us to extract lessons and then move forward. They are not there to be continually nurtured and embraced.

Consider this. The things, situations and people we embrace occupy sacred space in our lives, which means it leaves no room for the people and things meant to be there. I don't know about you, but this version of me refuses to miss out on who and what is for me. There is no time or space to hold on to expired situations.

So, we all have a choice. Either we shove our pain to the back of our emotional closet, or we purge it and make ample space for healing and growth and for the people who deserve a seat at our table.

Be Inspired!

Let's Get Intimate!

"Intimacy is not purely physical.
It's the act of connecting with someone so deeply;
you feel like you can see into their soul."

— Anonymous

I like to pay attention to relationships. And not just the romantic ones but all relationships. I often have conversations about their breakdown and the actual cause, and I think it's a way to learn and cultivate healthy partnerships.

Additionally, perhaps I have this desire to understand because I see how the landscape of how we date and nurture our romantic relationships and friendships have changed. I don't feel that everyone places the same value on them anymore.

Our relationships have become somewhat easy to discard and move on without much thought or reflection. It's almost as if we can't be bothered to work on them because it's possibly too much of a hassle, and we don't want to go through the motions of discovering and fixing the problem, which may or may not reveal that we are part of the problem.

So I thought I would do some of the work for us and identify an area that more than likely requires adjustment.

If we look at what is lacking in most of our relationships, we can say that intimacy is one of the most significant factors. And before our minds trail off into the bedroom, let's be clear that although intimacy does include sex, it's not ONLY about sex.

I love definitions and believe they set the foundation for understanding and gives us the ability to move forward in conversation, so let's start there. Intimacy is defined as closeness, a strong familiarity, or friendship. But I want to go a step further and include that outside of sex, intimacy has some other faces that we tend to forget, and I think they are the missing links in our relationships and friendships.

Let's look at the other faces of intimacy, they are:

Emotional – Can you be vulnerable with one another?

Intellectual – Can you discuss world events and differing points of view?

Experiential – Do you share your life experiences, both good and bad?

Spiritual – Do you have the same or similar belief system?

The commonality among all of these is communication, people! We need to be better communicators, myself included. We need to be willing to speak openly to one another without fear of repercussion. These forms of intimacy all require a level of vulnerability and openness. And I think the lack of some or all of the above is what is killing our relationships. It's almost as if we can only focus on one area of intimacy and can't seem to multitask, causing all the other areas to suffer. This leaves our relationship lopsided and unfulfilling.

Failure to confront issues in our relationships is a product of pride and the inability to choose a discussion over an argument. Toxicity chooses to argue because the individual wants to prove who is right and who is wrong. Maturity chooses discussion as a means to gain an understanding in an attempt to move forward. These are critical areas of communication where I believe we need to spend more time.

So I pose a question and a challenge. Let's think about individuals we are in close connection with and assess if intimacy and healthy communication is part of our relationship. If you are blessed enough to say yes, then I congratulate you. If the answer is no or kind of, then I ask if you are willing to do the work to ensure it becomes balanced?

I believe that intimacy creates soul connections. It goes beyond the surface and creates depth. When we explore intimacy, we attempt to dive into the inner workings of how we operate within the confines of our relationships and is beneficial to all involved.

I want us to have uncomfortable conversations with one another and slowly peel back the layers we all have. I want us to find a safe space for our emotions and create a place where intimacy not only resides but flourishes. I want us to get intimate for the sake of the longevity, quality and depth of our current and future relationships. Are you up for the challenge? If you are, where will you begin?

Be Inspired!

Week Ten

Are You Misunderstood?

"Be true to yourself, even if it's at the risk of being misunderstood."

— *Unknown*

Do you feel the need to explain and re-explain yourself in creative ways in hopes of being understood? Do you go as far as feeling responsible for people misunderstanding you? It's ok to say yes because I've been there too, and rest assured clarity eventually shows its face.

I am confident that we will encounter people through our lives who will always believe what they want about us and are committed to misunderstanding us. Plain and simple. And to recognize and accept this requires a level of self-awareness, maturity and depth of healing. It's also another tough pill to swallow, but you will realize its benefits once it goes down.

I have grasped that someone's lack of understanding has nothing to do with me or you but everything to do with their commitment to seeing things through a restricted lens with a partial perspective. It's not us; it's them! Literally!

See, as we grow, be it intellectually or spiritually, we begin to move differently. Sometimes our circles change, the books we read and music we listen to shifts. The conversations we have tend to affect us differently, and the things that inspire us are new.

We have the ability to step into old spaces with a new mindset and believe me, no matter how much you adjust, you are going to feel uncomfortable. It's going to feel as if you shouldn't be there. I encourage the feeling of no longer fitting into old spaces because it's a level of freedom everyone should experience at some point in their lives.

Unfortunately, as we celebrate taking up different spaces, there are people in our lives who want to force us back into the moulds they created because it keeps them comfortable. They want to put us back in the same box in which they met us.

They are the ones who continually say, "you've changed," or "you don't do this or that anymore." They won't admit it, but they are delighted to see us stagnant, just like them. And no matter how many times you try to explain, they don't or choose not to understand.

When I cared about being understood, I always wanted to paint a picture that people would comprehend. But now that it's no longer a concern, I can sashay away knowing I haven't changed. I've arrived and elevated.

The intent of this declaration is not to hurt, confuse or even be pompous. It just is what it is! And even those eternally committed to misunderstanding us will have no other choice but to accept the declaration for the screaming truth that rests between the lines.

Let's keep a few things in remembrance as we all move towards healing, living our truth, and elevating. Stand firm in refusing to live someone's idea of who you should be. We don't need to explain a changed mind. We don't need to clarify our very existence. We don't need to explain why we no longer laugh at the same jokes or read the same books. Heck, we don't need to explain why we changed our hairstyles.

All we need to do is decide to do it, become one with our decision and live our lives with purpose unapologetically.

Be Inspired!

Week Eleven

Decluttering The Chaos

"When we throw out the physical clutter, we clear our minds. When we throw out the mental clutter, we clear our souls."

— *Gail Blanke*

I have a confession. Clutter has a way of finding me sometimes. It's a confession because I like it when all of my hangers face the same way in the closet. Although they are not colour-coded, I organize my shirts from sleeveless to long sleeves, skirts in one place, dresses in another, and fold my jeans on a shelf.

I am the person who likes to organize the fridge with clear bins, so everything has its rightful place, and yes, the eggs are removed from the carton and placed in a separate container. I am proudly THAT person.

But yet I find that there are times every few months where things pile up a little bit in different areas of my home. And before I know it, I am overcome with disarray, and an item that generally has a designated place has managed to find a temporary home elsewhere.

Being an overthinker and deep diver in the why behind the things I do, I've concluded the clutter in my home reflects the chaos in my mind. So not only is my living space confused and in disarray, so is my mind. I understand my mental clutter comes from too many internal conversations and not enough verbal discussions with the appropriate individuals.

I would love to say that it's because I'm an introvert, but that is a load of rubbish and a complete cop-out. I am learning that I need to be more vulnerable because my lack of this essential tool fuels chaos. And since I cannot organize chaos and place it in a bin, I have no space for it in my life.

I have also realized that as much as I think my solo conversations prepare me for the real thing, it contributes to additional angst and clutter. I confess, and somehow, I feel better now that I am emotionally exposed!

I have tried tidying my physical space first but find myself spending hours moving items from one place to another, never progressing but rather running around in a circle. It's exhausting because I never manage to get around to handling the initial task.

Learning who I am has helped me in these situations to recognize that I need to deal with my mind and soul before I can tackle my physical space. You may need to do the opposite, and there is nothing wrong with that. The key is to ensure we sort out both areas no matter the order.

Misery sometimes loves company, so I hope someone out there is nodding and can relate on some level to the reality of the clutter and all that it entails.

The takeaway from this is easier said than done, but it's not impossible. To move through our emotional clutter, I think we need to clear our mental space and acknowledge the chaos that stands before us. Let's recognize that our mess, both physical and mental, is self-inflicted. I am sure we would love to shift the blame on a person or a situation, but this is totally on us. We need to own it.

Let's be open to moving through our clutter versus shifting it from place to place. Let's have uncomfortable conversations versus finding comfort in internal musings that offer no solution. Let's be willing to discard the chaos and roam free in an emotionally clutter-free zone.

Be Inspired!

Emotional Baggage Check

---

*"Everyone comes with baggage.
Find someone who loves you enough
to help you unpack."*

— *Unknown*

I love to travel, and I have an odd satisfaction when I hear the click of a stamp pressing against a fresh page of my passport. Travel provides a sense of freedom, and the only thing I dread is approaching the check-in counter to have my bags weighed.

You see, I tend to overpack because I love a "just in case" outfit. Fellow over-packers know what I mean. It's the outfits you know you won't wear but pack it "just in case."

I always make sure I don't put too much in my carry-on for two reasons, I want something light to carry, and I want to place it under the seat in front of me for quick access.

You see, I think we treat our emotional baggage similarly. Some we check-in and watch it move down the conveyor belt of life, then vanish out of sight and stay hidden for years. Then it resurfaces when we find ourselves in a relationship and have to claim it. Why? Because it is ours, and we have to claim it whether we want to or not.

Then, the more manageable baggage is strategically placed before us but doesn't require much attention. It's easy to ignore and contains the things we may need in a bind, so we keep it within arms reach.

When I speak of emotional baggage, I think of guilt, shame, fear, regret, etc. I believe these things result from any adverse experience we have encountered but never healed from entirely.

When it comes to our relationships, as important as it is for us to deal with the emotional baggage we have collected, I think it's vital to be with someone that is ready and willing to help us unpack while we are prepared to do the same.

I shared this thought with someone, and they said they were not interested in a relationship that involved helping another person unpack. Well! to say I was shocked is an understatement, and I attempted to have an open mind and understand from their perspective of not wanting the perceived burden of a partner's unresolved trauma. Maybe it's a personality thing. Perhaps it's because I'm an empath, but I couldn't find a way to agree with their view.

No matter how much work we individually do unpacking and healing from our stuff, there will always be leftovers. Even if it fits in a carry-on bag, tucked under the seat in front of us, it's still there. These things trigger us, and the hurt little girl or boy in us resurfaces and relives certain moments. Why? Because even though we heal, we still have scars, and there is never a point of emotional perfection, and that's ok because we can rely on the fact that there is dynamic growth in the midst of it all.

I am learning that vulnerability without borders is essential to our relationships. To properly unpack our baggage, we need to find the sweet spot of vulnerability first. I believe wholeheartedly that an additional ingredient to a healthy and thriving relationship or friendship is to be ready to share the load. If we are only willing to carry personal baggage, what is the point of the partnership?

I am a culprit when it comes to carrying multiple bags at once. I will go shopping and have another person with me but grab all the bags in the trunk, many cutting off the circulation in my fingers and arms. All while the other person is standing there empty-handed and perplexed.

You may ask, why do I knowingly struggle? And in full transparency, it's because I think I can handle it all myself. But the bigger question I need to ask is, do I have to? Do you have to?

Contrary to popular belief, we don't have to do it ourselves, provided we have the right person in our corner. We need to allow them to take a few bags from us to make the load more manageable, maybe even light. And on the days when our load isn't as heavy, we can take a few of theirs and share the weight. That is how our relationships with others are supposed to look, in my opinion.

Remember, our emotional baggage hinders us from trusting, loving and living fully. It keeps us encased by impenetrable walls and hides the parts of us that need embracing and shown affection.

Knowing this, I ask you to make yourself accessible to the eager person waiting to help carry, sort and empty your baggage. And lastly, remember, we didn't pack the bags on our own, so we shouldn't expect to carry and unpack them on our own, right?

Be Inspired!

Extension Of Grace

"Be Kind. Be Patient.
Be Generous. Be accepting.
Be all of these things to yourself."

— *Unknown*

I connected with an old acquaintance the other day, and she said something that inspired me to write this.

She eluded that being a parent is rewarding but has consumed her, which is not bad. I think it's beautiful that she immersed herself in parenthood in addition to her career. What stood out to me was when she said she is now "giving herself permission" to focus on herself. And as I reflected on her comment, I came to realize what a profound statement it was. It's not simply the act of focusing on one's self; it's the act of permitting yourself to do so.

I think we all need to adopt a similar mindset, not exclusively to those who have children but to all of us who are required to wear more than one hat. I feel it's a brave move, and I wish more of us would take the time to make that decision, not solely for the sake of our loved ones but for our mental health and the love of ourselves.

It's easy for us to put our heads down and get things done, day after day, simply because we have to. But the danger lies in the fact that ten years pass, and we finally look up, and we don't recognize where we are or how we got there.

Unfortunately, we get caught up in the throws of life and attempt to be all things to all people to the point of neglecting ourselves and losing ourselves in the process.

But rest assured, a day of reckoning arrives when we stare at our reflection and remember that we still exist as an individual. It's that moment we take off the hat of a parent, spouse, partner, friend, sibling, co-worker, boss and any other title we have and can call ourselves by our God-given names and stand naked in our truth.

It's scary because it's not often we take the time to face ourselves; it's even more terrifying when we don't recognize our reflection. But when we do, it's a liberating experience that no one can take away. It's a moment you never forget.

As humans, we tend to extend grace and forgiveness to those who have wronged us along this journey we call life, yet we have a hard time extending that grace and forgiveness to ourselves. It's fascinating because we are the only person on this earth who will never leave our side. Pause on the idea that of all the people in your life, YOU are always by YOUR side. Yet, we fail to give ourselves the grace, love and kindness we so readily offer others.

I want to encourage you to extend more than an arms-length of grace to yourself. Re-introduce yourself to the things you used to enjoy and do them often. Give yourself permission to breathe and take the time to reacquaint yourself with your reflection.

Be Inspired!

Do You Know Your Worth?

---

*"When you start seeing your worth,
you'll find it harder to stay around people who don't."*

— Unknown

I purchased a new vehicle not long ago, and when I asked the dealer what my old car was worth, they punched in a few numbers and told me $424. So to say I was floored is an understatement, and if I'm honest, I also felt a bit disrespected by the offer. I mean, why not a solid $500? But I digress.

Despite having more than 300,000 kilometres and a touch of rust, I knew it was worth more. I also knew that vehicle like the back of my hand. I knew how well I took care of it, both inside and out. I knew how much work had been done on it, not to mention what it took me through for 14-years. We went through a lot!

I refused the dealer's offer, had a conversation with God and donated my vehicle to a local non- government-funded organization that helps people who struggle with addiction. And instead of cash in hand, I received a tax receipt for well over $424. Talk about a win-win!

The moral of the story is not about making a profit. It's about me knowing what my car was worth and being connected to a group of people who shared my vision.

I watched a sermon by Bishop TD Jakes where he said, some people can't and never will see the treasure in you. And a light went off. He was so right. There are times when we allow the perception and opinions of others who tend to look on the surface, sully the reality of who we know we are. So, I say this from a place of love. Stop depending on others to build you up and determine your worth. Doing so gives them that same power to tear you down. You don't need anyone's validation to know your worth.

I have learned that there are two types of people in this world—those who see our worth and those who fear our knowledge of our worth.

Those who see our worth are the people who see us, encourage us, support us. They know what we are capable of when we are unable to acknowledge our capabilities. They are the people we don't need to convince to stay because they have decided in advance.

The ones who fear our worth or our knowledge of our worth are those who never see the good in us. They are the ones who pick us apart and remind us of past mistakes. They thrive on ensuring we continue to question ourselves. They see who we used to be, but not who we have become. I don't know about you, but I have a deep dislike for these people.

Someone once asked why some people are willing to accept the breadcrumbs handed to them in their relationships? Why are they willing to take being half loved and half appreciated? Why is the bare minimum ok? And the answer is two-fold. One is because they accept the crumbs as if it's all that's available, so they take what they can get. And two, they don't realize their worth and are unable to comprehend that they deserve the whole loaf.

I want you to remember that a crumb kind of love is not good enough for any of us. Understand that your worth is not up for debate or discussion because you don't need to prove your worthiness to anyone. Those people who are for you will recognize your worth without you needing to perform to prove it.

Moving on from things and people is a complex task but a necessary move to make. It's not that we don't value them. It's that we have learned to value and appreciate ourselves more.

We need to know our worth, surround ourselves with people who see us and have a growth mindset and the intentions of fueling us to grow with them and be better humans.

Something to remember this week:

"When you know your worth,
you don't have to beg people to like you,
love you or spend time with you.
Be confident in who you are.
Everyone can't afford the luxury
of being in your presence."

– Unknown

Be Inspired!

Week Fifteen

Open Up And Bloom

---

*"They were silenced until their
soul started screaming."*

— *Unknown*

I have an orchid with two buds, both of which are taking forever to open up and reveal whatever colours are inside. I am sure it has ample light and water, yet the buds remain closed. And what's frustrating is that it's been so long since she has bloomed that I can't remember the intricate design and colours she possesses, but I know she is beautiful.

Sometimes, probably more often than not, we can be like that orchid. We become complacent in the comfortability of our solitude and dealing with our pain as a covert mission that when it's time to be open and reveal our true selves, we have soul-numbing stage fright. It's the fear of what the other person will say or feel about what we share. It's the perceived judgement, and all of it seems overwhelming. It's scary!

Part of me doesn't see anything wrong with holding back to a certain extent because I advocate protecting your sacred elements. And I often need to remind myself that people can be in our lives yet not be granted full access. Now those of us who like to hold everything in are not off the hook at all. We need to be willing to lower our guard, embrace vulnerability and open up to the right people while remembering not to do so in vain.

What I mean by the latter of that statement is that some people want you to open up because they seek information. We all know someone like this; they want to know for the sake of gathering information to share with others. They are just plain ol' nosey!

Some want to act as your therapist and psychoanalyze you, while others want to treat you like a project and "fix you." Then we have those whose intentions are pure. They are my favourite kind of people because they are seasoned listeners who have the main objective of understanding us. They are the people with whom we can have intimate, unforced conversations. Not many of us have this type of person in our lives, but when we find them hold tight. They are rare.

"I see you" are three powerful words standing between a bud and a full bloom. People that "see you" peel off the layers and see us and accept us as we are. Perfectly, imperfect.

They are the ones who are a consistent force in your life and patiently stand by as you muster up the strength to permit yourself to trust again, and when you do, they are first to lend an ear as you open up and allow everything to flow out of you like a gentle stream. They are also there to celebrate the unexplainable peace that follows your awakening.

I love this week's quote because it emphasizes what happens internally when we finally allow ourselves to be open. It's that moment where silence transforms into a faint whisper, and slowly its volume increases and is more audible, and the more one opens up, the louder their soul becomes, to the point that it screams. Not from a place of anger or frustration but a place of freedom.

I acknowledge we can all be like my orchid bulbs, some of us more than others, for various reasons, but maybe all it takes is time and the right environment for us to open up and show the beauty dwelling within us all.

Be Inspired!

Sunshine State Of Mind

"We can't truly yearn for something until we feel the effects of its absence."

— *@theinspiredintrovert_*

When the sun is shining, life tends to look different. Colours illuminate, and what seems unimpressive on a cloudy day possesses a certain depth and beauty when the sun shines.

The sun makes my soul bubble, and it puts a permanent smile on my face. It elevates my mood and injects me with an energy I can't seem to explain.

When I penned the above quote, they were words that flowed, but as I pondered them, many things came to mind. First, we can't miss the sun until we feel our energy change and our mood shift from the lack of having it.

We can't miss the warmth of its rays until we feel the coolness of a constant grey sky.

And as much as we love the sun's effects, we need to recognize that the things we have cleaned on gloomy days do not appear as clean as when the sun is out. We see streaks on the mirrors, a light film of dust on the hardwood, and the stainless steel has the dreaded fingerprints we thought we removed.

The sunlight manages to illuminate all the things we miss and amplifies what's hidden in the shadows. It's similar to the exposure of the unhealed parts of us as it whispers that although we have come a long way, there is still some work to do.

On the other hand, when the sun hovers over areas, we are sure we didn't clean properly; we are often surprised there isn't any dust or residue. That's similar to the situation we encountered but never imagined we would recover. But here we are, flourishing, living and loving.

I don't think we can truthfully miss the closeness of connection until we have experienced the void and hollowness of loneliness. It's almost like many of us need to experience emptiness before we can value and appreciate being full.

Let us develop a new appreciation for sunny days, not just for the fantastic selfies, but also for its warmth and the things it reveals. Sunny days show us what we need to work on and illuminate how far we have come, all because we've taken the time to recognize how we feel when it's not there.

Be Inspired!

Week
Seventeen

Ultimate Quest To Wholeness

"Seek to be whole, not perfect."

— Oprah Winfrey

I'm a whole woman. I mean, I'm a whole lot of woman with all this body I have, but I am whole nonetheless. And as always, I have a question. Why is it that when we are single, we somehow see ourselves as half a person? Scratch that, even those in relationships sometimes see themselves as half a person. Declarations like "waiting for my other half" or "you complete me" imply we are not whole, and I must admit these statements make my curious mind wander.

Let's first agree that two halves make a whole. And if we seek a love relationship or are in a love relationship with the idea that our mate is our 'other half,' are we not just left with two incomplete people invading one another's space?

When you go to a restaurant and order something, you expect a full plate with everything mentioned in the menu description. And if you don't get it, you are annoyed and send it back to receive a new dish with everything described. Correct?

If so, why are we willing to accept half a person when we won't accept half a meal? Why aren't we setting the exact expectations in our love relationships as we do at a restaurant?

When you are whole, you deserve wholeness in return. I think the only way to do that is to change the language surrounding the idea of seeking someone to complete us and become complete far in advance of allowing another person into our heart space.

Perhaps it looks like knowing who we are at the core of our being, not how others perceive us. Maybe we need to write down everything we know is true about ourselves and walk in that truth unapologetically. Perhaps we need to cultivate a stable relationship with ourselves before we invite another person to the party. Let's get comfortable sitting at the table alone while we figure ourselves out.

Those of you already in a relationship, you're not off the hook, nor are you stuck. You have the opportunity to curate a relationship with yourself, and when you pull back the layers, a whole person will emerge, and you may be surprised at what you discover.

I want to leave you with this: The issue with society is not a relationship issue; it's a singleness/individual issue. From our youth, society programs us to believe that life's natural progression is to be in a love relationship, and that will make us complete. It implies that we are to marry before we turn thirty, have a few kids and live happily ever after. Nowhere does it encourage us to know who we are in advance of those things, should we even want them. Please note that getting married and having children, the above is an option, not a pre-requisite for a fulfilled life.

This next part is in my humble opinion. Attempting to be in a relationship or continue in one without discovering who you are in the process will result in two individuals who are strangers to themselves trying to get to know one another. And until we embrace the beauty of singleness and knowing ourselves, our relationships will always be where we seek fulfillment but find emptiness. So take the step and begin your quest to wholeness. Once you start, nothing and no one can stop you!

Be Inspired!

Stop Faking It!

---

*"Being fake is the new trend,
and everyone seems to be in style."*

— Unknown

I took out my braids one day, and my hair needed some serious TLC. The problem with my hair was that I also had errands to run and could not go out looking like I just returned from battle. So I grabbed a scarf and tied my hair in the cutest wrapped style, did my make-up, and went about my day. The moral of the story is that I was put together on the surface, and no one knew the complicated, dirty disaster under my headscarf except Jesus and me.

We live in an age where social media is the breakfast, lunch and dinner of choice. It's a place where people cover the embarrassing and untidy parts with filters and carefully created videos. They are primed and proper outside searching for likes, follows, comments and compliments.

Still, once the façade fades and their nakedness is revealed, I wonder how many dare to acknowledge their brokenness. I wonder how many people find it easier to concoct a new plan to cover it up tomorrow as they struggle internally with unresolved trauma.

When I checked Google today, the world has about 8 billion people, and there is only one of you, so I must ask, why would you want to be like anyone else? We have gotten so used to faking it until we make it; it's no wonder when it's time to get to the root cause of our pain and sort out why we are the way we are; there is silence. We fail to see where fiction ends and reality begins.

We put so much stock in blending in and caring what others say and think that we neglect the necessary time it takes to figure ourselves out. It's almost as if we would rather bury the pain and hope it dissolves into oblivion. But we have forgotten that just because we bury something doesn't mean it's dead!

When we plant and water a seed, our intentions are for it to grow into something useful. If we think of our hurt in the same context, our untreated and ignored trauma may operate similarly. It's buried, watered with resentment, anger and unforgiveness and grows, but unfortunately produces more hurt, more pain, and the inability to move forward. And dare I say, it negatively affects our relationships and their ability to thrive.

Personally, I would much rather have the scar of an old wound that reminds me of where I have been and how I used to feel than one that is open and oozing with a hurt that festers and never heals. We can spend years ignoring and covering our pain with a fake smile and outward appearance to the point it becomes a full-time job ensuring it never gets to the surface, but let me make this crystal clear, buried pain can't heal until it's unearthed.

I wonder why we are so afraid? Is it having to experience the uncomfortableness of dealing with the pain? If it is, rest assured you are not the only person with that fear, and you most certainly won't be the last.

I can promise you, once you have allowed yourself to feel the gut punch, pricks and stings of unearthing your pain, there is freedom and peace on the other side as the wounds heal. You may even have the audacity to ask yourself why you didn't face them sooner!

If I could describe the experience of letting go and allowing yourself to feel all the feelings, I would say it's like the warmth of the sun on your face after weeks of cloudy skies. It's like when you first step from dry land into the ocean and feel the waves crash against your ankles. It's like melting into the embrace of someone you haven't seen in a while.

I challenge us to use the same energy of maintaining our façades and apply it to remove our masks bravely. Let's make the first person we have a heart-to-heart conversation with be with our reflection.

Be Inspired!

Week Nineteen

Who Pours Into You?

"I water you, you water me, we grow together."

— *Brandon Nembhard*

Watering cans are useful when filled because their sole purpose is to give and receive. We are like watering cans because we often spend an immeasurable amount of time pouring into others to the point of depletion and emptiness. What we forget is that what is empty eventually needs to be filled. So I ask, who is pouring into you?

Maybe you are someone who has no problem pouring out, but when it's time to be replenished by another soul, you have difficulty receiving. In full transparency, I am the person who doesn't always openly receive as much as I give, and as I do the work to allow myself to receive, I want you to attempt to do the same. I also want you to be open enough to know that accepting help is not a sign of weakness or evidence of lack and should not be seen as such, nor should it be viewed as a transaction, but rather recognized as a sign of strength and an act of both kindness and love. I think it's important to note that our willingness to receive is a firm reassurance to our helpmates that we trust them enough to assist us.

Do you have tunnel vision with your outpouring? Is your sole mission in life to help others but not be helped? If you are that person, perhaps you need to be open to the idea that we all need to acknowledge that unhealed hurt, trauma, and mistrust act as a lid on our vessel. It stops us from receiving the very thing meant to sustain us—the thing we need but fail to realize.

You see, when we refuse to allow people to pour into us, we deliberately stunt all areas that assist in personal growth.

But once we remove the proverbial roadblock, we will see other like-minded vessels standing on the sidelines, patiently waiting for us to heal and remove our lids, so they can pour into us and keep us replenished and full without question or hesitation. I challenge you; better yet, I challenge us that as we openly give, we have the same openness to receive the goodness other vessels want to pour into us.

Being poured into requires a level of vulnerability and our need to set aside our pride and understand that we don't need to do everything ourselves. We are not created to live in silos but are naturally designed to be partners and communities who help one another, especially within our relationships. As I write this, I want you to know that as much as I encourage you to shift your thinking, I encourage myself to do the same.

I have learned that it's essential to pour into the right people but what is equally important is that we come to a place where we can remove and heal from the things hindering us from receiving.

Let's allow people to pour into us for various reasons. One reason is that we are tired and can't always pour into others. The second reason is that there are people in our lives who are eager to pour into us, and we need to allow them to do so. Let's prepare ourselves to be vessels willing to receive as much as we are eager to give.

Be Inspired!

Week
Twenty

The Plight Of The Strong
Black Woman

---

*"Be soft, do not let the world tell you,
all you can be is hard."*

— *Unknown*

I have been talking to some of my girlfriends lately just about life in general, and the more we spoke, the more I realized that there was a trend. WE ARE TIRED! We said it, we own it, and we will repeat it until we don't have to say it anymore.

I read a quote that added salt to an already tired wound, and I didn't know how to feel about it until I sat and let the words permeate. Soon the calm contemplation turned into a moment of controlled rage coupled with many questions. It read: "A strong Black woman doesn't let a tear stain her face." But why?

These words are possibly why when you ask a black woman how she is, many of us will generally tell you that we are tired. And that tends to end the conversation or take it to a place we didn't intend for it to go, with suggestions of lavender on a pillowcase or a long hot bath and a massage. Let me be honest with you; sleep cannot and will not cure the type of tiredness we are experiencing. Our SOUL is tired, and if any of the above could heal a weary soul, there wouldn't be a reason for this post.

You know her, the head shaking, finger waving angry, rude, stubborn and overbearing black woman. Yeah, that one! And let me throw in the word aggressive because I know many black women who have been called aggressive at some point in their lives and careers for merely speaking up for themselves or voicing their concerns. I wonder if anyone understands the destructiveness of that word and how it contributes to the weight of our tiredness.

On the other hand, we are strong, the shoulder to cry on, the problem solver, the advice giver, the prayer, the force to be reckoned with, the defender and the list goes on.

But what about the woman who resides at the core of who most of us are? The delicate part of us. The portion that, unfortunately, is considered out of 'character' when quiet and calm? And God forbid she shed a tear! I'm here to tell you we are not playing a role. As much as we keep going, it doesn't negate that we are running on empty, and the fumes are slowly choking the life out of us.

The black woman is expected, whether blatantly or covertly, to be all things to everyone, always to have a stiff upper lip and shake things off. And the term I often hear is "you'll be fine, you're strong," but we have to understand that amid our strength, it can't last forever.

Strength requires replenishment. We need to change the narrative that "A strong black woman doesn't let a tear stain her face." It's not a trophy; instead, I see it as a death sentence wrapped in a compliment. There are two types of tired. One requires sleep, and the other requires peace. We need both. So let's normalize the black woman as delicate as much as we normalize her as strong. Why? Because WE ARE TIRED!

Be Inspired!

Week Twenty-one

Chit-Chat & All That!

"Love yourself enough to set boundaries…
You teach people how to treat you by
deciding what you will and won't accept."

— *Anna Taylor*

Today is a good day for a bit of chit-chat. Who am I kidding? Every day is a good day for chit-chat! I have this friend, and when we get together, our conversations go from foolish where we can barely contain our laughter to chats so deep neither of us knows how we got there. We always manage to touch on random topics. One day, in particular, we focused our energy on speaking about trauma, boundaries and the fact that we have given normality to the things that destroy us.

We talked about the fact that we sometimes endure unacceptable behaviour based on what we saw growing up and who exhibits the behaviour. I accepted the notion, but in my true nature, I needed to know why? So I took to the streets. Well, not the street, but I sent a voice note to others in my circle and posed the question.

You know you have good friends when they entertain your random questions late at night or far too early in the morning. One of them said that when we willingly receive unacceptable behaviour, we must remember two things: the person exhibiting the behaviour has unresolved trauma or was raised by someone with unresolved trauma, and neither knows any better. Another said that some people are just disrespectful and realize it and don't care.

Then the response that left me undone was posed as a question. They asked, "what is missing in us that we see the treatment as the standard, to begin with?" And I pose that question to you because I think it's worth pause and careful contemplation.

There's that saying that if you know to do better, you should do better. So, where does that leave us? I understand that unhealed trauma and baggage filter into future relationships, but do we continue in the cycle of transferring trauma from person to person and generation to generation? Do we continue to excuse it away and say we are a product of our environment? Maybe we need to continue changing the narrative and do our due diligence by opening our mouths to have the necessary conversations that will work towards healing, not just ourselves but also those with whom we have relationships.

Something else that came up in conversation was why we recognize red flags and unhealthy patterns and justify ignoring them as the best way to cope? And I share this next part as insight because someone made this point not long ago. Just because you may share DNA, living space, or even a bed doesn't permit another person to treat us unacceptably.

Read that again because that statement is the naked truth. The more I discussed this with different people, the more we realized the solution lies in the necessity of setting boundaries in our friendships, family relationships and love relationships.

Our boundaries are not about the other person; it's solely about preserving a sacred space around ourselves without constructing a wall. It's the ultimate form of self-preservation that more of us need to practice if we are ever going to make it in this ever-changing world where people's sense of entitlement in our lives is at an ultimate high. Setting a boundary is becoming comfortable saying no without explanation. It's also stopping and letting individuals know that how they speak to you or treat you is unacceptable. Setting a boundary is sticking up for yourself.

Let's recognize that giving negative behaviour a new name doesn't change the damage it does. Let's also acknowledge that just because we played in the sandbox as kids, run in the same circles as adults or even share a few similarities in DNA does not automatically give people access to you. It also means that if someone receives the gift of entry into our lives, they are not immune to revoking that entry.

So here's to calling out bad behaviour and not giving it a new name to make it more palatable. Here's to using our voice and shutting down people's audacity to be disrespectful. Here's to healing from our trauma and the trauma that was transferred to us unknowingly. Here's to setting boundaries in all facets of our lives. Here's to an open mind and an open heart, ready to receive whatever comes our way.

Be Inspired!

Week
Twenty-two

Authenticity & Approval

"Never trade your authenticity for approval."

— *Unknown*

We sometimes alter who we are to align with others' wants and needs and find ourselves creating a balancing act of who we are versus who they want us to be. We are consistently shifting ourselves to make others comfortable, be it in our family units, love relationships or work environments. We alter how we speak and interact to make ourselves more palatable and digestible. We nod and say yes when we want to scream a resounding "heck no!"

I can't remember what movie it was, but the line that stuck out to me was this: Within our authenticity lays our most significant power. Let that sink in for a moment. No one is you, and no one could ever be you. God created one of you, and if that is not a foundation to maintain your authenticity, I don't know what is.

I am not sure if my introverted ways or personality cause me not to be bothered with keeping up with others. I mean, I struggle enough to stay true to myself. I can't take on the additional task of trying to be someone else. I used to be asked to attend work functions. I would always say no because forced interactions make me highly uncomfortable, and just because everyone else was going was never a reason for me to attend. As a result, my decline would be brought up in performance reviews year after year as if attending functions was a job requirement. And I would plead my case, year after year. Then finally, I put my foot down and said my no, was a firm no, and to stop expecting me to step outside of who I am in an attempt to appease the masses.

You see, sometimes we need to put our foot down and be true to our reflection despite how uncomfortable it may be in the moment or for the other person looking on. They will eventually adjust to the authentic version of you. We are not for everyone, and I think moving through life will be much easier when we realize this and accept it.

Being true to ones-self is the only task at hand. Look yourself in the mirror every day and remember who you are. Remember that you are exquisite and carefully created to be one person and to do so authentically.

I may have mentioned before that I am naturally drawn to real people because I can see them for the glorious mess they are. They are the ones who don't come polished and shiny but instead are bruised and crumpled but always real in their true authentic state. Those are my favourite people, and I wouldn't trade them for a different version.

I want us all to aspire to be our authentic selves without worrying about what other people will say or think, because let's face it, as long as people are roaming this planet, they will always have something to say anyway.

Be You and Be Authentic, and while you're at it, Be Inspired!

Week
Twenty-three

It's Time To Break Free

---

*"The biggest challenge in life is
to be yourself in a world trying to make
you like everyone else."*

— *Unknown*

We live in a world where there is a fine print is associated with the perceived freedom to experience and speak our feelings. I believe there is an underlying disclaimer for us only to share how we feel as long as it doesn't shift outside the lines of the pre-conceived notion of acceptability. We are "free" to express as long as it aligns with how others feel. And don't dare have the audacity to express those feelings outside of those confines because someone may be offended by your truth.

Does anyone else see how ridiculous the above is? And because of this level of absurdity, I refuse to blend in. I resist! We should never let being ourselves cause us to roam this world with a closed mouth.

There is no prize for adhering to the confines of the status quo. It's boring there, and God created us uniquely and wonderfully for a reason. I don't understand, nor will I ever understand, why everyone wants to be the same. Is there comfort in being like everyone else, thinking like everyone else and feeling just like everyone else? If there is, I choose to be uncomfortable, unique and interesting. I choose authenticity over anything.

Do you find it challenging to create a balance between logic and emotions? I ask because we can sometimes become caught up with wanting everything to be aligned and make sense in our heads that we don't give our souls adequate space to feel. In my humblest of opinions, maybe we need to embrace the feelings of angst and uncertainty when it presents itself as much as we cling to feelings of happiness and joy. Perhaps this will allow us to recognize these feelings in advance because they will inevitably show themselves in the future, and only then will we have the freedom to call them by name.

Have you ever been all in your feelings? You know it's the times you cry watching movies or as you express yourself to a loved one. I think it's our bodies responding to the feelings that overwhelm us. One minute you're laughing and the next crying, not due to sadness, but because you are going through the emotions versus suppressing them.

I want to challenge ourselves to unlock the vault of our feelings and recognize and accept them for what they are. Why? Because there is mysterious freedom in allowing yourself to feel, and maybe it shouldn't be such a mystery but something as familiar as talking about the weather or sports. Perhaps we need to speak our feelings with the normalcy of everyday conversation.

May we be free to be as we are. May we be free to say what's on our minds. May we be free to feel all the feelings and express them in our way. May we be free to speak when we want to talk and be silent when we so choose. May we be free to let our yes be a solid yes and our no be a definite no and not desire or feel pressured to explain. May we be free to be ourselves.

Be Inspired!

Week Twenty-four

How True Are Their Colours?

"When someone shows you who they are, believe them."

— *Maya Angelou*

Have you ever noticed when you are amid an altercation with someone, they tend to morph into an unrecognizable being? It's like a real-life Dr. Jekel and Mr. Hyde. They somehow find the most hurtful words to say to you and speak in a manner you have never experienced, and when it's all said and done, you aren't sure if what transpired was real or a figment of your imagination.

In these moments, the other person provides you with a front-row seat to witness who they are, and they present you with the opportunity to choose whether you want an encore performance in the future. I have often heard it said that you know a person's true character when you are in the midst of an argument and hear the words that come out of their mouths. What they say is what they mean and how they act is a testament to their true character.

The following is strictly my opinion, but I feel that a few of you may agree. The things a person says in the heat of an argument is a glimpse into how they feel about you. And knowing this, I wonder if the excuse of "oh, they are just upset" is valid. I question whether a shift in mood and inability to control both their temper and tongue is a good enough reason to accept intolerable behaviour? For me, it will always be a no, and I hope it's the same for you. And let's remember the cliché of all clichés, which is also true. How a person treats you and speaks to you is a reflection of what they think of themselves.

It would be negligent to only look at this matter from one perspective, so let's flip this idea entirely and place ourselves in the presence of someone gentle, kind and considerate even in a disagreement. They are the one who listens intently and speaks respectfully even when they are upset. They never call us out of our name and find the words to discuss rather than argue.

I bring this person up for two reasons. One because they are mature, and we all need this level of maturity in our relationships, and two because after spending so much time with the unstable Jekel and Hydes of our past, we rarely give the breath of fresh air the credit that is due.

Are you wondering why we do this? I think it's because we use the dysfunction of former relationships as the blueprint for our future relationships. When we do this, we end up in the same relationships repeatedly with the same types of people. When the kind, considerate and consistent soul enters our space, we don't know how to accept them and receive what they have to offer. We have conditioned ourselves to equate the dysfunction as standard rather than ease into the calm of respect and peace. We have become accustomed to and possibly addicted to toxicity.

I want us to re-evaluate the state of our relationships. First, let's trade the rollercoaster Jekel and Hydes for stability and the freshness of consistency. Let's give up the ghost of mistreatment and learn to embrace the treatment we deserve. Because when someone shows you, they are a jerk, it's true, but when someone shows you, they're specifically created for you; believe that as well.

Be Inspired!

Week
Twenty-five

A New Perspective

"What you see depends not only on what you look at but also on where you look from."

— James Deacon

Do you ever forget where you are? I'm not talking about your address or GPS location; I mean where you are in relation to where you used to be.

I consider it a lapse in memory or maybe even a refusal of perspective, and I find myself searching the four corners of my home and sometimes have a hard time pinning down my location. The pandemic had me going from one set of pyjamas in the morning to a comfy jumpsuit in the afternoon and a fresh set of PJ's in the evening. It's a sad state of affairs come laundry day, as my baskets are filled with comfy "home" type clothing as if I never leave the house.

I decided to search for the who and where of myself today. I did my hair, gave myself a facial, manicure and pedicure. I changed out of my track-suit and opted for pants with a zipper and shoes with laces. The details are significant because everything as of late has been elastic waist and slip-on shoes, lol. Anyway, as I emerged from my bathroom, there stood a forty-something-year-old me, and at that moment, I remembered who I was and where I was.

Perhaps you have similar eureka moments when you take the time to permit yourself to recognize where you were versus where you are current-ly. This is especially true for those who have been on a journey of healing and emerging as new versions of themselves. I find it interesting how easily we forget how things used to be compared to how they are currently, and I'm not sure if it's the same for you. Still, I like to look back to see how far I've come, especially on the days where I find myself in survival mode, and I am going through the motions but not experiencing them.

Sometimes we can get caught up in the mundane tasks of work and life that we lose sight of who we are outside of those roles and locations. We make a conscious effort to check on the whereabouts, be it their physical location or the state of their mental health and well-being of others, but how often do we check in with ourselves? We often become so busy on the round-about of life that we lose sight of the direction we are going and where our journey began.

You see, I don't think we can appreciate the journey if we lose sight of where it all began, and it's imperative for us to take the time to stand outside of our current dwelling place in life and mark off where it started, where we are and where we want to be. Doing so provides the necessary perspective required and acts as a gentle reminder that we are doing great.

I think it's natural for us to spend an enormous amount of time focused on where we are that we often refrain from looking at the past in fear of dredging up the negative, and we rarely find the courage to look ahead in fear of "jinxing" the good that may come our way.

But what if we changed our interpretation of what each of those places represents and used the past as the journey's starting point. Then as we live, grow and heal, we can see and measure our progress with confidence. We can see all of the hurdles we have cleared and the valleys from which we emerged. And let's not stop there. Let's not fear looking forward but rather be open to everything that has yet to come our way.

Here's to acknowledging the past, living in the present, looking forward to the future, and never losing sight of the entire journey.

Be Inspired!

Week
Twenty-six

Just Breathe

"We can't enjoy anything while holding our breath."

— *Unknown*

To date, many of the pieces have been heavy, and I am not apologizing because I think they are all necessary for us to feel deeply and process those feelings. But I will give you a break this week, so inhale and then exhale and get ready to breathe.

Can we take a moment to shout out the people who have given us a reason to smile again? They make an effort, not for reciprocity but simply because it's their desire. They see us as we are. They love us as we are and appreciate the things we never thought were worth appreciating. They love the parts that we fail to see as loveable. They see the cracked and broken bits of our past and help us reinforce the seal to ensure we are held together. They embrace us as the perfectly imperfect individuals we are.

The very thought of telling someone how you feel makes one nauseous. The idea of sharing secrets and uncovering our hidden parts can make one want to run for cover. But then boldness emerges, and we do it anyway. I don't want us to take for granted those who dare to love again and have the audacity to do it with sweaty palms and racing hearts.

Kudos to those who have found a reason to live, but this time with purpose and grace. To those who have found a reason to trust again and attempt the journey of loving and living one more time, I offer admiration.

Can we take the opportunity to realize the level of nerve this entails and how petrifying this unchartered territory is when you are resurrecting from a place of hurt? A round of applause and endless "I'm so proud of you" goes to everyone who is and will experience the release of forgiveness and the joy of moving forward. Although it's not easy, it is required for your complete healing.

So go ahead and the time to acknowledge who you were, embrace who you are and brace yourself for who you will become because although change is inevitable, it's also a journey that requires acknowledgement. As we write, read and speak our way through to a place of healing, everything becomes clearer. So Breathe!

Be Inspired!

Week Twenty-seven

Soul Recognition

"Be so connected;
your roots become entwined."

— *@theinspiredintrovert_*

When I thought of this quote, I instantly imagined a large tree with thick, strong roots entwined to the point of not knowing where one begins and the other ends.

I think about humans in the 21st century and realize that so much of what we encounter takes place on the surface, which can be beautiful; still, I wonder how deep our roots extend and if they have a firm footing in our connections.

We are a society that desires comfort but lacks genuine connection. Perhaps if we took the time, we would realize there is something unique and beautiful about unforced conversation and unexplainable connections.

I crave deep connection over anything. I wouldn't say I like large gatherings because there is no space for intimacy amid a crowd. I'm not too fond of small talk either, as it tends to remain on the surface, and my psyche desires more. Nothing gives me a tremendous sense of anxiety than forced interactions. It makes me want to crawl under a rock and succumb to any other form of pain. Yes, dramatic, but an honest feeling of internal agony nonetheless.

When a person enters my life, and the conversation is easy, like a stroll on the beach in summer, I am in a state of bliss, and my inner eye roll morphs into a twinkle, leaving my brain stimulated and happy.

Don't get me wrong. I embrace silly interactions and conversations about frivolous things submerged in nonsense. But I know with the right people, those conversations will inevitably dive into the deep waters of the meaning of life, our purpose and the fact that no two stars in the sky are the same. And above all of that, we can comfortably sit in the beauty of silence when required.

Have you ever met someone, and you instantly connect? You know, it's as if you met before and were picking up where you left off? Yet you never set eyes on them before your first meeting? It has happened to me twice in my life to date, and although those individuals have a special place in my heart, it was and still is quite weird! I think about them one minute and get a text or phone call from them the next. If that's not a connection, I'm not sure what is.

As humans, we like to dissect things and attempt to understand the whys and hows in our lives, and because I'm inquisitive and I know many of you are also, there is satisfaction in the revelation. But what if there isn't a solid answer for our why in this instance? You see, I don't believe in coincidences, but I do have confidence in the idea of divine interventions of souls that connect far in advance of meeting in the flesh. And believing this, I wonder how different our relationships would be if we gave space to chance connections, threw logic out the window, and embraced things as they presented themselves. What if it didn't have to make sense for it to work? What if you could look at each other, shrug and just be happy you connected and move forward?

I want you to embrace the idea of soul recognition. It's the idea that sometimes souls recognize one another before the physical bodies meet. So when you find a soul that effortlessly connects with yours, don't sabotage it, don't dissect it and please don't discount it as too good to be true. Embrace it for the mystery that it is and go with the flow. Open minds and open hearts can lead to the start of something unexplainably beautiful if we take the time to step out of our way.

Be Inspired!

Week
Twenty-eight

Discovering An Ongoing Freedom

"Time is the beautiful friend of healing."

— *@theinspiredintrovert_*

Have you ever watched one of those romantic comedies where a couple breaks up, and it's usually the female who goes through the motions of "getting over" her lost love? Let me set the scene. Too many bottles of wine consumed, too many drunk texts and phone calls to the ex ranging from anger to uncontrollable sobbing and one panicked phone call to her friends and support system. The night ends with her phone confiscated and endless tears over a makeshift bonfire, burning everything that reminds her of him. And scene!

Not every relationship ends that way, but I needed to set the stage. I see the bonfire as a sign of purification, and getting rid of the old makes space for the new both mentally and physically. But there is always one item we tend to keep either hidden or in plain view for various reasons. It could be out of melancholy, necessity or just because you like it.

Whatever the reason, I know there is a part of us, actually let me speak for myself; there is a part of me that is often haunted by said item. I think we all do it to some degree, and I wonder if we have recognized that parts of us are still tied to old situations. Let it sink in because this was a revelation for me as well.

I parted ways with an item that weighed about 2600 pounds that was a subtle yet very loud reminder of my past, and it wasn't until I signed the papers to release it that I felt a new sense of freedom. I had no idea of its burden and how I was tied to it until I decided to remove it.

It's like the skin of a popcorn kernel that's found its way beneath the gum of a tooth. Most times, it's in the back molar, and your floss can't reach it. Your tongue manages to find its way back there at the most inopportune moments, and no amount of flossing, brushing or rinsing releases the kernel skin. Then suddenly, you get it! There is a release, and your tooth is finally free from the annoying thing that was a constant reminder of last night's popcorn.

You see, we often need to let go of things to become better versions of ourselves, but there is often a reminder. Knowing this, I have learned that there are levels to freedom. There is a misconception that once you are "free," there is nothing else to concern yourself with, but I think this is incorrect. We move through levels as we heal, much like the bonfire, and then there is that epic level where you're standing at the peak of a mountain, knowing you conquered the obstacle. An unspoken reassurance accompanies the final stage of freedom: nothing can resurface and shake us because we are no longer bound. Our physical and mental space is open, and our hearts have that much more room to receive.

I say all of this because I think it's essential for us to reassess our surroundings often to ensure there aren't things and people lurking in the background of our minds and hearts keeping us bound. These are things that hinder our growth and stop us from resting comfortably in our final stage of freedom wherever they may be and with whomever those moments are with. There is nothing wrong with it taking time because time is the beautiful friend of healing. If I can extend something that may help, it is vital to identify your triggers because failing to do so keeps us bound in past hurt.

Lastly, what's important is that we move through it all with patience, grace, and a celebratory shout when we finally let go. That's when lasting freedom can show its beautiful face.

Be Inspired!

Week Twenty-nine

Love & Appreciation

---

*"Everyone wants to be loved,
but how many desire to be appreciated?"*

— *@theinspiredintrovert_*

When was the last time someone said they appreciated you? Perhaps it's been a while, and you need to go into the archives to dig out that moment of affection, and that alone should be a reason to pause and ask why? How do you feel when someone says they love you versus when they say they appreciate you?

When someone says they appreciate you, I feel they see all of you. They see your hidden bits and pieces. They almost dig for them as if looking for that rare diamond. They notice your annoying habits and your greatest and not-so-great qualities, yet through it all, they still see you and appreciate you. They take the time to acknowledge how you make them feel when you are together and sense the absence of those feelings when you are apart. They take all the things that make you, you and embrace them. I am speaking of appreciation in your family unit and friendships, and because I can't help but touch on romantic relationships, I am also zeroing in on that. I feel we tend to get caught up in being in love that we forget the necessity of being appreciated within those relationships.

The definition of love is said to be a strong affection for another person arising out of kinship or personal ties. Affection, on the other hand, is a feeling or expression of admiration, approval or gratitude. Personally, just because someone says they love you, it doesn't equate to them appreciating you.

Rest assured, I am not discrediting the necessity of loving another person and being loved in return. Still, I am questioning the lack of appreciation in the nooks and crannies of our relationships. I am also curious about the level of desire we have to be appreciated. I told a friend that when someone I care about tells me they appreciate me, it hits a different part of me because, as I said earlier, to appreciate me is to see me. To appreciate me is to know and acknowledge me as more than a vessel that gives. I also think that when someone tells you they appreciate you, they see the things in us that we don't clearly see in ourselves. And that brings me to another question.

Could it be that appreciation is not on the top of our list of requirements because we don't appreciate ourselves? I ask because if someone were to tell me they appreciated me a few years ago, I would have said thanks and walked away without absorbing a single word or thinking about what it meant. But when things shifted in how I saw myself, the phrase "I appreciate you" means so much more and warms my soul.

This makes me think there is a possibility that we don't see the validity of appreciation from another person because we don't value what we possess as individuals. There are people in our lives who appreciate things about us that we don't see for ourselves and until we start appreciating ourselves, we won't have the capacity to embrace it.

I want you to remember something. When someone says "I appreciate you," please know that person values the things you may not view as unique. When they acknowledge you for the things that come naturally, it speaks volumes about how they feel about you and illuminates a power within you. There is purity in that.

When someone takes the time to utter those three magical words, they give you space to acknowledge and appreciate yourself. It's an eye-opening experience and is a great teaching moment in self-acceptance and self-appreciation.

So I want to leave you with this thought and something you can ponder when you think about love and appreciation this week. **To love me is to have affection towards me, but to appreciate me, is to see all of me.**

Be Inspired!

Week
Thirty

Do You Have
The Capacity To Love?

―――――――――――――

*"Some people are in love with the idea
of love but may not have the capacity
to give or receive it."*

— @theinspiredintrovert_

―――――――――――――

Let's talk about the word capacity for a moment to put things into context before we dig deep. Capacity is the maximum amount that something can contain in its depth or breadth. It's the amount that something can produce and is also the ability or power to do, experience or understand something. So I ask, how much capacity do you have to give and receive when it comes to love?

We have probably all seen or been in a situation where a woman or a man ready for a relationship finds themselves in a partnership with someone who doesn't have the depth to receive the magnitude of love they have to offer. Perhaps they don't have the depth to receive what someone is offering, and unfortunately, the result is one individual ends up dissatisfied.

When I have conversations with people, I like to know what type of relationship hurt they have endured. How much unresolved trauma and past hurt are you willing to hold on to, and at what cost? I ask because I think this is something we rarely ask ourselves or those we are in a relationship with despite it being one factor that hinders our relationships. Healing from our wounds allows us to move freely in a world designed to keep us bound.

"We have an unlimited capacity to love.
The only thing that limits our capacity to love
is the conditions we place on love."

- Unknown

I was thinking about what gets in the way of us receiving love, and I believe a lot of our lack of capacity comes from damage from prior relationships and failure to face our demons and heal before we move on to something new.

Our ideologies on how something should look versus allowing it to flow freely make our love relationships stagnant. Lack of self-worth and feeling that we don't deserve to be loved is a roadblock that hinders all progress. The list goes on, but what's most important to remember is that we are in control of our capacity to give and receive, and when we recognize this superpower, we will be free.

When we emerge from a place of pain and find ourselves in a position to love again, I think we need to be careful with whom we align ourselves. I say this because we need to ensure the other soul can receive the volume of love you have to give and vice versa. The right person at the right time will be able to receive the abundance of love you have to offer, and you, in return, will have the capacity to accept what is reciprocated.

There will be a time when we are ready to love, which is a scary but exciting place to be, but before you jump in with your heart and arms open wide, it's essential to ask if the love you are ready to bestow upon another soul is one that you have for yourself. We overlook self-love because we think another soul has the power to love us enough and make up for the love we have failed to give ourselves, which is the furthest from the truth. But once we master the art of self-love, we are in a position to receive outside love in return.

This is critical because we forget that love is a two-way street, but it begins with ourselves. There is a misconception in that phrase where we think it means we love someone, and they love us back, and we live happily ever after. But we miss the life-altering exchange, which is turning that love inwards and only then will the circle of love be complete.

So I challenge you to have the capacity to love yourself fully, love another soul and be open in breadth and depth to receive the magnitude of love waiting to be extended to you.

Be Inspired!

Week
Thirty-one

Awakening A Stagnant Mindset

---

*"Until you change your thinking,
you will always recycle your experiences."*

— *Unknown*

When things lay dormant, they lose their ability to operate as designed. They are inactive, and development ceases. Items begin to break down and become fragile to the touch. They collect dust, grow mould and run the risk of being deemed useless.

I saw a quote the other day that said people like to see us through a lens of who we were, but not who we are. And the older I get, the more I find this to be true. I wonder why people can't see us as we grow into better humans. Why can't they allow us to evolve and celebrate that growth with us?

Why are people so committed to seeing us how we used to be? It has come to the point where it feels like they want to hold us hostage as the former version of ourselves.

I find it very disheartening to see individuals grow and blossom into a new version of themselves and listen as they converse with friends or family who are unfortunately eager to bring up the past amid a present disagreement. I don't think I will ever understand the mindset of using our past as a means to maim and chip away at the newer versions of who we are. It is not a constructive form of conflict resolution; instead, it damages the individual on the receiving end and the relationship.

People with no character development frighten me to the core. How can someone be the same person they were twenty years ago with no change to their mindset or their growth. Someone asked my opinion on something, and I thought about it and said what I needed to say. They then turned and reminded me of what I said about twenty- years ago on the same topic and pointed out the difference in my response.

I was baffled that the expectation was that my opinion on a matter would be the same twenty years later. A part of me was offended because having the same opinion would imply they didn't expect any change or growth in my perspective over the years. But then I realized they had a stagnant mindset, not the other way around.

I want us to continue asking ourselves difficult questions and digging into why we do things, and react the way we respond in certain situations. I want us to be uncomfortable as a means to enhance growth in all areas of our lives. I want our opinions on situations to shift as we mature mentally and spiritually. I want us to evolve into the best versions of ourselves that we can be while we continue to inhabit this place we call earth. And I want us to do it all unapologetically.

Why? Because some people won't let us forget who we used to be or what we used to do. They won't allow us to forget how we used to act or react to certain situations. They intend to keep us confined to our former identity and attempt to stop us from becoming who we are destined to be. They are comfortable holding us hostage in the past, and if you aren't aware, they are not our people.

I desire that we continue to change and get better. Twenty years from now, I expect our mindset to be different because we will all have an additional two decades of life experience under our belts. As long as we grow and our mind is elevating, we are moving in the right direction.

Be Inspired!

Week Thirty-two

Visiting The Past

"Forgive yourself for the nonsense
you entertained when heartbreak
made you forget who you are."

— *@drthema*

Have you ever wanted to go back in time and slap yourself? Have you ever looked back at situations and question both your intelligence and sanity? And then you realize who you are is not who you used to be. The person of days gone by didn't know who they were and, therefore, didn't know how to handle things like the person of today does. And that should give you pause. You see, I think we need to understand that past missteps, poor decisions, heartbreak and everything in between had to occur for us to rest in our current space.

Unfortunately for many, being treated poorly needed to occur to learn and understand the power of forgiveness. Not forgiveness only for those who did us wrong but forgiving ourselves for allowing certain things to happen.

It's in our nature to think about seasons past, and I don't think we can stop ourselves from going there, nor should we. But I think we have to ask our intentions for a visit before making the trip. Because the past is there to remind us how far we have come, and it has the power to help us heal, but remember, you don't live there anymore.

When I visit the past, I try to have moments of reflection and not moments of regret where I beat myself senseless over the head with questions of why I didn't see things sooner and when the red flags were waving and covering my face, why did I choose to ignore them? You see, regret is a stumbling block, and I believe it is tightly woven with shame. These two things are the enemies of progress.

Regret and shame cause us to keep looking back so far that we lose focus and trip over old situations. We reinjure ourselves causing a setback to our healing. Regret is much like picking at a scab repeatedly, never allowing the wound to form new skin, therefore, exposing it to the destructive elements of shame. Doing all of this interferes with our progress and healing.

Now, visiting the past isn't always doom and gloom; there is a flip side. I realized that we sometimes associate the past solely with our negative experiences, but let's agree our past wasn't all bad. We rarely visit the excellent times and act as if they never existed or were not impactful in shaping part of who we are. We shake hands with trauma and embrace pain and disappointment but rarely have deep conversations with happiness and joy. It's not often we sit back and hang out with laughter and peace.

I wonder why that is? Why don't we visit the good times? Are they not just as important as the bad? Do they not have lessons like the bad times? Have we slowly morphed into martyrs who only find comfort in sorrow?

I used to regret the day I met the person who hurt me and but once I recognized who I was, I realized that although their brokenness caused my hurt, it was necessary for my healing. There is that saying, "the straw that broke the camel's back," well, that last occurrence of pain was the last straw required to break me before the building of a new mindset and new life could commence.

Please understand that the past doesn't need to focus on the negativity and pain, but try to pick out moments of joy to create balance. Your past is about where you were versus how far you have made it, and don't forget it's also about where you're going.

If you are at the beginning of your healing journey, the past more than likely still makes you quite angry. There are oceans of unforgiveness and mountains of confusion combined with many questions that you will get through.

If you are in the middle of your journey, your past is a place where you have regret and shame and find yourself in a mental tug of war between being over it and still upset by it.

If you are at the end, you are more than likely in a place where you can speak of your past with reflection and possibly slight humour. You can easily find the lessons, call them by name and acknowledge where you need to take responsibility.

Frankly, they are all great places to be because what stands out is that there is dynamic emotional movement. So take some time, congratulate yourself on where you are going and ensure you nurture the good times as you learn from and move past the bad.

Be Inspired!

Week Thirty-three

Please Read The Label

---

*"Our instructions need to include
both what to do and why it is important."*

— Belinda Letchford

What would be the state of our relationships if we all came with care instructions which would help our relationships thrive and remove all of the guesswork that comes with cultivating sustainable relationships.

They would be like the care instructions for our clothes or warning labels like household cleaning items. Think about the number of times you have picked up a garment at the shop and put it down or returned it because it was dry clean only, or wash by hand and lay flat to dry.

I know as soon as I see cold water tumble dry on low or hang to dry, I get excited, and anything other than that makes me contemplate if I want to commit to the additional care it requires.

What if we all came with labels such as, be decisive because she lacks patience or please handle with care; he's overly sensitive? Wouldn't it be something if our labels instructed us to communicate effectively to avoid unnecessary misunderstandings? And my favourite, respect is required at all times, even when mad. Empathy is required, contains unhealed trauma and matching baggage.

What if we also came with warnings? Caution, they will continuously be on your mind. Brace yourself; acts like a child when in an argument. Danger doesn't take responsibility for their actions. May cause uncontrollable smiling for no apparent reason. I mean, the list could go on, and we would all know what we are committing to in advance. Talk about an emotional win-win!

If we want to wear silk, it has to be dry cleaned or washed by hand and cared for delicately. We have to recognize the responsibility of having such a delicate fabric in our wardrobe and accept the care it requires.

The same goes for our relationships. If we want someone in our life who is solid, with whom we instantly connect on all levels, we want to not only maintain that feeling, but we want to expand them to heights unknown. We both need to take responsibility and nurture one another so the relationship remains authentic and intact.

Unfortunately for us, we don't come with labels, and neither do our mates, but what we do come with our hearts that feel and mouths that speak, and I suppose if we are willing to be vulnerable, that is the label we all wear. Vulnerability allows us to take the time to get to know our mates and understand them in their entirety. This includes celebrating with them when they are happy and on top of the mountain and sitting beside them in the valley as we attempt to understand how they cope when stressed and how we can move through those moments with them versus hiding out until it passes.

How committed are you to get to know your person or the people in your life? What lengths are you willing to go to in an attempt to understand them in their entirety?

Effective communication requires comprehension, and comprehension requires deliberate and active listening. We need to listen to gain understanding, and understanding requires levels of patience. None of this will be easy, but I am confident it will be worth it. Let's spend more time digging into the crevices, peeling back the layers of the ones we love, and creating more moments of harmony and authenticity.

Be Inspired!

Start Expecting

"PUSH: Pray until something happens."

— *Unknown*

Have you ever prayed for something, and then when it happened, you were shocked?

I am laughing as I write this because it happens all the time. First, I am shocked, followed by many questions about the very thing I prayed about. Now, I know it sounded insane when I went over this in my mind, but now that it's in print, I confirm the level of insanity.

Why do we do this? Why do we second guess the reality of what we said we wanted or needed? And I notice we do this in our relationships. We ask for certain qualities in a mate, and when we align with someone who has them all, plus many bonuses, we have the audacity first to question it and then say it's too good to be true.

I mean, really? Did we not just ask for this? Did we not just spend all these years healing from foolishness to get to a space of embracing goodness, joy and everything in the middle? Did we not just do all the groundwork and wait patiently for the big reveal? The answer is yes to all of the above. So I ask, why are we hesitant when we get it?

Do we not believe that we are good enough to receive this blessing? Do we not trust the giver and provider? Do we think we can do better on our own? When will we remain in the process? When will we pray, step aside and wait and be open to receive?

You see, we get the first two after much practice but drop the ball on the third. We are not preparing ourselves to receive, and it's not because the provider has failed us; instead, we aren't expecting; or prepared accordingly. It's like trying to fly internationally without your passport. You won't get very far.

God is not a genie, nor should we treat Him as such, but when we do pray and ask for answers to those prayers, I think we should do so with a spirit of expecting and if it doesn't' happen, understand that either it wasn't meant to be or it's just not the right time. Things I prayed for years ago are happening now, and I believe they are taking place because I can receive them with a right mind and a grateful heart. My focus has shifted from self-sabotage to basking in the glory of celebration.

So to all of those questions I posed above, I encourage you to spend some time thinking about each of them and analyzing your current situation.

No matter what you believe, I encourage you to start expecting, even if you think it's out of reach, dare to step out in faith with open arms to receive with not only a grateful heart but an expectant one.

Be Inspired!

Week Thirty-five

Move In Love & Forgiveness

"You have to forgive people
who sometimes aren't even sorry.
Master this, and the blessings will overflow."

— *Unknown*

I have a little bit of food for your soul today that I stumbled upon, and I needed to let it sit and come to fruition on its own accord.

The idea of moving in love will be different for everyone and may require some reflection, but when something moves me, it stirs an unknown space in the depths of my soul. It's one of those things that you feel but cannot explain. It just is.

There is so much here that I want us to take apart and put back together. Some of you will apply it to a specific period in your life; many may set it aside for later use, while others may discard it. The choice is always yours. As children, our parents and caregivers forced us to apologize when we did something wrong, but as we grew up, the apologies became fewer. We find reasons why our behaviours are justified, and apologies rarely show their face.

We have all felt the sting of hurt, the slap of deceit, the embarrassment of being taken advantage of, ridiculed and mishandled in so many different ways. But through it all, there comes a time when we need to learn to accept apologies we never have and will never receive.

For the longest time, I never quite understood the whole idea of forgiving without an apology. It seemed ludicrous because I thought I needed a firm apology complete with a few tears and much pleading, that was until I had to set all of that aside and put into practice the idea of forgiveness without apology. I get it now.

When hurt enters our space, the first reaction is to get revenge in any possible way because you want that person to hurt as much as you did. And we don't want them to walk away as the perceived winner in the situation. None of us wants to go down without a fight. Right?! But no matter how many things you try, there isn't any satisfaction and what's worse is that sometimes while you are waiting for the floor to fall from beneath the one who hurt you, they seem to be doing just fine in life infuriating us even more. I really dislike this for us.

But I come to you from a place of insight as this is as real as it gets. If I were to sit and wait for someone to apologize to me for what they did that almost destroyed me in every sense of the word, I would be waiting a lifetime in misery. It came to the point where as much as I wanted the apology, I knew I would never get what I wanted. So I took matters into my own hands, and instead of seeking revenge, as much as it would have temporarily satisfied the rage inside me, I chose to forgive without an apology. I decided to let God handle that person in His timing.

Once I conquered this, it created the space I needed to forgive myself, which is the most important thing. I never understood how much power there was in forgiving myself, but I have learned and experienced the immense space it offers to live and love without shame, guilt or regrets. I realize that we cannot forgive another person until we forgive ourselves and heal from our wounds.

When we shift our focus from pain to healing and, most of all, focus on forgiveness, things look different. And maybe that's precisely how moving in love is supposed to look. Remember that the gift of forgiveness is one we give to others, but we also need to unwrap it and present it to ourselves before true healing can take place. May we all have peace of mind and the ability to move in love and live flourishing lives with or without the apology.

"Forgiveness does not change the past,
but it does enlarge the future."

– Paul Lewis Boese

Be Inspired!

The Responsibility Is Yours

"Do not look where you fell
but where you slipped."

— *African Proverb*

I'm not sure how many of you will like me after this, but I'm ok with it because we both know it's coming from a place of love.

It's good to feel all the feelings, correct? But do you think we sometimes use our feelings and what happened in our failed relationships as a means to avoid giving ourselves the constructive criticism required in regards to our participation in the demise of our relationships?

It's essential for us to feel and understand our feelings from all sides, but what is equally important is taking the time to look back and see where we went wrong. You see, we have to take some responsibility for some of the things that happen to us. There are situations where we are innocent victims, and then there were situations where we were willing and active participants. The latter is where I want to go back in time and sort myself out, and you may want to do the same.

It's uncomfortable, and no one promised it wouldn't be, but if we want to live a thriving life, we need to take responsibility for many things we have encountered. I also think we need to take an honest look at our role in our suffering to heal completely.

I believe it's vital for us to examine how we could have handled past situations and how we could have responded to many circumstances differently because we don't do it enough. I don't think we reflect on our participation in some of the dysfunction in our lives.

I am the first to admit that I am apologizing far more than I ever have before in this season of my life because I am learning to be self-aware, and let me tell you, it's hard! Because when you are in the process, it requires a level of humbleness where deliberately apologizing is necessary.

I am learning to step back and place myself in the other person's shoes and examine how things could be interpreted and let's just say I am wrong a lot, but I am also not afraid to admit it. I am not scared to pick up the phone and say, "Hey, I was wrong and what I said or didn't say wasn't fair." Because of this, I have reflected long and hard on my participation in the dysfunction I have encountered. Once we can acknowledge and take responsibility for our involvement, it will be easier not to repeat toxic patterns and enter toxic relationships and friendships. Sometimes, it's us and not them.

I have said this before, but I like to ask people what they learned from their last relationship. I ask because the answer speaks volumes. It says whether or not they take some responsibility for where they could have gone wrong. It will reveal a level of maturity, desire to grow, and desire to do better.

We are not glossing over the responsibility of others and how they treat us because that definitely comes into play, but we do need to step back and see where we are responsible. (this does not include abusive relationships; those are of a different realm)

Our responsibility lies in acknowledging, recognizing and illuminating the areas we lack and doing better as individuals. Simply put, no one wants to redo past situations with new people. No one wants to have part two of pain. The only way to avoid going through the same terrible cycles is to acknowledge what we have learned, which will stop us from attaching ourselves to people who are not for us while checking ourselves in the process. So let's take responsibility to a new level as we heal one day at a time.

Be Inspired!

Week Thirty-seven

In The Midst Of Fear

---

*"When you choose to let fear keep you
in your comfort zone, you might think
you're avoiding failure. What you're really
doing is choosing failure in advance."*

— *Luvvie Ajayi Jones*

I had a dream that shook me from my sleep in a panic. My heart was racing, I had sweat moistening my upper lip, and my breathing was laboured. Perhaps it was a panic attack, but whatever it was, it woke me and kept me up for the rest of the night. At that moment, I recognized the power of dreams and how they can shake our reality to the core. I also recognized the power of fear while awake and in a deep sleep.

In this dream, I walked to the top of a steep hill to catch the sunset. When it was over, I turned to descend, and the terrain was much different from when I ascended. I was somehow much higher and felt as if I was at the peak of a mountain. Every direction I looked in seemed impossible. The fear of falling had me paralyzed, and I envisioned hitting every body part on the edges of the rocks, and I froze. It was getting dark, and I could see other people making their way slowly down the hill with no problem but there I was in my stupid flip-flops, stranded. I turned around and noticed a path I hadn't seen before and somehow had the sense to abandon my flip flops, steady myself on the very rocks I thought were going to maim me and make it to the bottom of the hill. The reason I paint this picture is that our perception can be deceptive.

We are often so caught up in the doom and gloom in our heads that we can't see the forest for the trees, or in my case, I couldn't see the path amid the rocks. And it isn't until we get out of our heads that we can see things for how they indeed are with a clear lens. In this dream, all I needed to do was take off the stupid flip-flops, brace myself against the rocks and put one foot in front of the other.

I am learning that fear will keep us in a place far from reaching our fullest potential. It will keep us from telling someone how we feel, applying for a job or asking for a raise. It will keep us stagnant, perched on the top of a hill like a spectator far away from living.

I still can't put my finger on the significance of the flip-flops, but maybe they symbolize the people in our lives that want to keep us stuck or are waiting for us to trip and fall, and we need to proceed in life without them. They are the ones who plant those seeds of doubt in us and support a limited mindset rather than encouraging us to do better. Whatever it is, I am sure it's something to ponder.

We will always find a reason not to make the descent into the unknown, especially if it requires us to take an unfamiliar route in uncharted territory, all while adjusting our perspective. Perhaps the things we see as obstacles are the very thing we need to lean on for leverage. Oh, and take off those stupid flip-flops!

Be Inspired!

Week Thirty-eight

Speak Life!

"Words have [power].
They can either bring the greatest happiness
or the deepest despair."

— *Sigmund Freud*

As much as there is power in our thoughts, let's spend more time under-standing the power of our words. The focus isn't on how something is said solely but also on the words we use.

When you have a moment this week, go back to week six, entitled It's You vs You, where we discussed the conversations we have with ourselves. This week's inspiration is along the same lines. Although we need to speak well of ourselves, we also need to communicate well and speak life into our situations and ask, actually no, demand that others do the same.

Have you ever had someone speak negativity into your positive space, and instead of walking away thinking you weren't affected, you find yourself replaying what they said in the back of your mind and what was clear is now murky? What was once a feeling of optimism is now bleak, and you feel depleted. These are also the people who manage to get you when you're already down, and instead of picking you up from the mire, they verbally keep you stuck.

I think we have all encountered these people at some point, and for some reason, we keep them around using the excuse that it's just the way they are or they are family, so you can't possibly ask them to leave you alone for the rest of your life. Perhaps they are not happy in their lives and feel the need to share the negativity.

I don't think we can expect vibrancy from our relationships if we consistently speak words of death into situations and people. When we say things like "He is never going to change," or "I'm never going to find love," we have literally spoken death on the situation and have earmarked it for failure. We fail to realize that as much as our words have the power to grow and elevate, they have equal power to kill and destroy.

I have some advice for you that I cautiously put into action for myself—be careful with whom you share your "stuff." Examine who they are, their intentions and what state their life is in before you share and seek advice. Ask yourself if their advice will help or hurt your situation. Often, the assistance you get from people isn't always coming from a healthy place or a healthy mindset and let's face it. Not everyone wants to see us win.

I remembered going to someone for help a long time ago. Had I known then what I know now about the importance of seeking suitable sources, or in my case, listening and believing my gut, I could have avoided a lot of unnecessary struggle. They were not in a good place for themselves, so I ended up enlarging my already open wounds by asking for advice from a wounded soul.

Another little bit of advice is to keep the intimacy and issues of your relationship between you and your mate. We don't need third-party commentary, which is not only for the sake of privacy but also for your mental health and the health of your relationships.

I find it interesting that the state of someone's life can filter into the trajectory of your life, so it's important to keep areas of your love relationships sacred. On a personal level, the only third party in my relationships is God. Once we take words more seriously, we will be slower to speak and more careful to react.

Do you remember the words someone says more than how they treat you? Words have a way of sticking to us, and have you noticed; negative comments have a knack for sticking to us more than positive? It's interesting, considering they are coming from the same source.

I think this is because our words are in a state of poverty. I say this because we are a generation of people who have difficulty expressing themselves and struggle to find the right words to say. We are a generation who rarely take the time to taste and digest our words before speaking, and meaningful and impactful, life-generating conversations are a thing of the past.

Let's make a point of surrounding ourselves with people and being individuals who speak life into us. We are not seeking confirmation that everything will be perfect; it's about being a support system offering advice and suggestions to increase growth. It's about knowing when to speak and when to remain silent. It's about speaking life and understanding the immense power in every word we speak.

Above everything, I want us to develop the habit of speaking life into our partners, family and friends. Tell them you care about them. Tell them you appreciate them. Tell them you are proud of them. Life-giving words create abundance, bring us closer together and help to grow and maintain lasting connections.

Be Inspired!

Week
Thirty-nine

Insecure, Sure & Unsure

"Confidence is Silent; insecurity is loud."

— Unknown

It's no wonder, but I like to pay attention to human behaviour and interactions, and a thought came to me, and I wonder if how I feel is relatable.

Some days I am sure about everything and walk in confidence. Other days I am unsure about everything and overthink my way to confusion, and in between those days, I have a touch of insecurity. But regarding the latter, I have insecurities that were never mine in the first place, meaning they were projected towards me and imposed upon me without me knowing and probably without the other people knowing.

I'm not too fond of some areas of the skin I'm in, and I am working on it because I love myself. But there are other things I don't particularly appreciate because people and the ominous "society" chose to imply that I shouldn't embrace that part of myself.

I'm sure most of these implications were whispered during my formative years in the most "helpful" of ways, and others were made during the years where I was an adult, but not a friend to myself, and because of this, I want you to do me a favour and join me as we mentally go back in time.

How far you go back is entirely up to you. But I'd like you to think about how you see yourself and how you feel about certain parts of yourself, be it physical or intellectual and separate the things you naturally don't like versus those implied, over the yeard.

Are you surprised by the number of implied insecurities you possess? Many of us haven't taken the time to think about them in this context before, but it was beneficial for me. Much of what we dislike about ourselves has nothing to do with us. But, everything to do with another person who decided to knowingly or unknowingly plant a seed of doubt in our minds. Now it's up to us to separate and undo those toxic thought patterns so we can move forward and live our lives embracing every part of ourselves no matter what others think.

I think there is power in the separation of what you know is true about yourself versus the perception of others. Often the harmful and hurtful things people say about you have nothing to do with you as an individual but more to do with them and their level of insecurity.

And I don't think we can come into that power until we first love and accept ourselves as is and second move into a place of self-awareness where we recognize the truth in the good and not-so-good things about ourselves. Once we get to that place, we can acknowledge that what one person doesn't like about us or sees as a flaw will be the very thing another person adores. For this reason, I believe that the negative opinions of others shouldn't hold as much weight as we allow them, no matter the source.

Have you ever been called intimidating? If you have, I am sure it bothers you. Perhaps it stemmed from giving your opinion that wasn't favouring the masses, or it could be because you have firmly said no to something others thought should have been a yes. And from those interactions and being called intimidating enough times, you not only start to believe it, but you become uncomfortable in your skin and adjust who you are to convert into something or someone more palatable.

Then eureka! Through extensive soul searching and separating your truth from perception, you realize the perpetrators used the character damaging word to wound you as a means to deflect from their insecurities. It's not that you're intimidating. It's that they wish they were able to speak their mind with confidence. Who knew?!

We can't discuss insecurity without mentioning society and the "beauty standard" and what they, whoever "they" are, consider to be acceptable. I think this is a classic example of implied insecurity. You see, we are told that beauty and intellect look a certain way, but what that means is that anything outside of what society has constructed as the "standard" is deemed unacceptable. How can we see that as logical in a world of billions of people of different races and genetic design dwelling in billions of bodies? Yet, we buy into it and forget that our bodies and intellect are not up for debate.

Let's stop allowing people to tell us what is acceptable and not acceptable. While we're at it, let's no longer allow those same people to take opportunities to speak mediocrity into our lives. Why? Because the more we try to fit into the mould, the more we will hate what we see in the mirror, which will continue to be the detriment to our relationship with ourselves and will inevitably filter into our love relationships. We have worked too hard to preserve both to go down without a fight.

Be Inspired!

Week
Forty

From Misery To Joy

---

*"Some moments are temporary shelters,
yet complacency has made them
a permanent residence."*

— @theinspiredintrovert_

Do you realize every time we choose to remain upset, we are making a deliberate decision to forfeit peace for misery? I have a new understanding of the whole concept of Joy, and it may or may not resonate with you. For the longest time, I thought I was joyful, content and happy, but I was miserable in every sense of the word.

You may wonder how one can confuse the two, so I will share a few things I have recognized along the way. We can have a form of joy because a smile, nice outfit and a dose of sarcasm can hide a multitude of pain, but on the inside, in the depths of our souls that refuse to speak, we can be miserable. And it's never just one thing; it's usually an accumulation of pain and unresolved trauma.

We have to acknowledge our misery and make an effort to see what was on the other side of it. We all have to be willing to call it by its proper name, and it is at that point where we will understand that misery is a place we visit now and again, but it's not a permanent dwelling. It's not home.

Do you keep a journal? I highly recommend you consider it a form of active therapy and a means to get out of your head if you are one to over-think. I sometimes go back and read old entries for perspective, and let's say, I can be a glorious mess at times.

But what I noticed in my entries is that I tend to journal more when things aren't going well, but when things are going well, I barely journal and the entries are short. I'm talking about the date, time and "I'm happy," and that's it.

As I recognized this, I challenged myself to deliberately journal when things are going well and do you want to know something? I find this so difficult and couldn't understand why. Then I concluded that misery is the friend who has overstayed their welcome, but we find a reason to keep them around for company. We keep feeding them and give them a warm place to stay. They then invite regret, confusion, second-guessing and ungrateful-ness into our space, and before you know it, you're consumed by unwel-comed guests.

Misery went from being a sole visitor in our home to a permanent res-ident living rent-free in both our heads and our hearts with the audacity to bring friends. Misery is the freeloader that we have permitted to take advan-tage of us.

Misery is like having a bath where the water is too hot, but you sit down anyway, and despite the heat piercing your skin, you eventually become one with the pain. Somehow everything becomes bearable because you accli-matize to the discomfort.

Many of us don't know how to receive joy or bask in its goodness be-cause we've allowed it to be foreign for long. We patiently wait for an in-terruption or a red flag. We tiptoe around, waiting for the floor to drop from beneath us, and when it doesn't, we are surprised and enjoy it briefly but find misery lurking around the corner.

When this happens to me, I chastise myself because I know better and need to do better. I keep myself in line by reminding myself that joy is good, happiness is good and feeling good is GOOD! I deserve it, and so do you.

These days, I find myself smiling on the inside because my soul is happy and feels free. It's not to say I don't have days where misery creeps in and takes a seat beside me because it happens. The difference is, I greet misery, then I quickly show her the door. On the other hand, Joy and happiness can come into my space, unpack and linger for as long as they want because their company feels good. They have the key and the security code to my space because I want them there. I need them, quite frankly. They are my balance.

As we transform into renewed versions, let's acknowledge that happiness and joy are always within our reach and should be welcome to reside with us on a full-time basis. Misery, on the other hand, will pop by, but its stay is limited because we all have better things to do with the life we've been given.

Be Inspired!

Week Forty-one

For Love's Sake: Part One

"To love you correctly, I first need to know how to love myself."

— *@theinspiredintrovert_*

I want us to ponder the following questions for a short while. What if the solution to fractured and unsatisfied love relationships was to love ourselves with an intensity and level of unconditional surrender <u>before</u> we attempt to extend that love to another person? What if we were to heal from past relationships, work on ourselves, and have a clear picture of what we want and need from another person and what we have to offer before entering into a new relationship? Consider it a sabbatical for the soul.

Next, I want to ask this. If a love relationship breaks down and you find yourself single again, do you have enough love for yourself to be ok on your own? We don't deny feelings of hurt, sadness, and everything in between because we're human, but will the level of love you have for yourself be enough once the pain subsides? Will you be able to step away wounded but not broken? If we can honestly say yes, then I think our hearts and minds will be in a position to receive a future love that is explicitly designed for us.

When I think of pure romantic love, I see it as something present throughout the seasons and travels through the rollercoasters of our lives. I don't think this type of love will ever cause you to question your worth or what you have to offer. It's the kind of love where the other person's deepest desire is to understand you to the point that your silence speaks volumes. It's respectful and reciprocated. It won't be perfect, but it will always be transparent and pure.

I envision some of you rolling your eyes and thinking, "Aye, nice try, but this is far-fetched," but hear me out. If we logically think about it, that kind of love is attainable. But first, maybe we need to love ourselves similarly before recognizing and receiving it from another person.

I'm not sure if any of you have completed the 5 Love Languages quiz, but I highly recommend it. I did mine years ago when I was fragments of my current self and re-did the quiz again when I became this new version of myself, and my results were staggeringly different. It was to the point I thought I made a mistake and took it two more times, just to be sure.

See, that alone was a revelation. I believe how we feel about ourselves and our level of self-discovery and self-acceptance reflect how we want and expect to be loved. Maybe the golden ticket is that when we know who we are and how we need to be loved, we will inevitably connect with the person designed for us without question or hesitation. We won't settle for anything or anyone that doesn't align.

One last thing, and it may sound cliché, but I am a firm believer in the necessity of friendship at the foundation of our love relationships. Friendship isn't just about the ability to laugh and be silly together, although it's crucial. It's also about being vulnerable enough to share our dreams, failures and deepest fears. Our partners need to be our peace, and we need to have a sense of emotional security when we are in and out of their presence. They need to be the place where we can share our stuff without repercussion.

Let me ask you this. When you remove the surface from your current love relationship, what is left? Is there a solid friendship there, or are you staring at a familiar stranger? No judgement, just asking because I think it's something important we have to ask ourselves.

There is a quote by Brandon Nembhard that states, "I water you, you water me, we grow together." And I am in love with the whole premise behind these nine words.

Why are we tangled in our love relationships if we are not nurturing them with a growth mindset? Why are you taking up a collective space if your mate is not your biggest cheerleader and vice versa?

If we can't or choose not to encourage and love one another to the point of exponential growth in our money, souls, and love for one another, that translates into us no longer moving in the same direction. How stable is a love relationship if we can't walk side by side?

I'm a hopeful romantic and a firm believer that everyone deserves an unwavering love relationship. It will present itself differently to us all. My only wish is that we are all prepared and recognize it when it shows its beautiful face because it will probably catch us off guard and won't follow a specific formula.

Let's not allow time to dictate how it all works out either, but understand we will know it's real because it will just feel right. There won't be any questions or confusion, just ease and a breath of fresh air.

Here is to celebrating and nurturing self-love, mending current love relationships and preparing for the love that is on its way.

Be Inspired!

This week check out the 5 Love Languages quiz at www.5lovelanguages.com

For Love's Sake: Part Two

"Hurt is not a prerequisite for a lasting connection."

— *Unknown*

As a continuation of last week, I want to remain on this theme, and a few new thoughts have come to mind that I wanted to ensure I gave careful contemplation.

I saw a quote on Instagram, and many people liked it, but the message troubled my sometimes sensitive spirit. See, the premise behind this quote was that you know you're in love and that it's going to last if you first go through hell and high water and remain together.

Although some of that may be true, it also implied that love couldn't show its face in the first place without a struggle, which is where I disagree.

We live in a world where we are conditioned to believe that struggle is required in advance to experience love and joy. It's almost an all-or-nothing mentality.

And I want to share that prior struggle or ability to withstand said struggle is not required for a sustainable love relationship. Maybe we need to step outside the dysfunctional normal and venture into a different direction. Perhaps we need to find comfort in revolting against the status quote in an attempt to build healthy, loving, long-term relationships.

I am not naive to think there won't be disagreements in relationships because as long as we have two humans inhabiting the same space, there will be friction. Still, I believe when we have friendship combined with healthy, open and mature communication, those disagreements will be short-lived, and love will continue to flourish in ways we may have never experienced without those components at the foundation.

Someone in my circle asked me why I am so hell-bent on pushing friendship as the foundation of love relationships, and I laughed and explained that I'm not a pusher. I am passionate and want to see all people invest in healthy, thriving relationships.

We often come up with dozens of things we want in our love unions but leave friendship out of the equation. I think it's because we don't see friendship as being a significant if not critical component. After all, it seems too simple. I equate it to cooking without salt. Salt is a simple ingredient that enhances the overall flavour of a dish, and without it, your food is bland, but with it comes life and unexpected depth. Friendship is that salt. Now that we have that sorted, I have another question to ask. Have you taken the time to examine what you have to offer in your relationship?

I ask because sometimes we can be selfish and only focus on what WE want out of a relationship that we fail to ask that fundamental question.

Let's face it, being pretty or handsome is nice, but it's not enough. As much as I want someone who will provide a safe place for my emotions, I must be willing to turn that around and examine if I can be that safe place for my mate. See, it's great to have the list, the standards, or whatever you want to call it, but we have to bring something to the proverbial table if we expect our relationships to be healthy and flourish.

I want to leave you with a few thoughts to ponder this week. Understand that not everything in our lives needs to start from a place of pain to mature into something extraordinary. Sometimes things are just beautiful from the start, so let's embrace goodness and nurture it.

Also, let's take the time to cultivate solid friendships as the foundation of our love relationships because I genuinely believe that the return on this investment is priceless.

And last but not least, I need to challenge you. Take the time to look at the list I know you have, which indicates all the things you want from your current partner or future partner and then see how you measure up to your request. I'm sure we all have some work to do. Remember, love has to start somewhere, so why not have it start with you?

Be Inspired!

Week
Forty-three

Breaking Down The Walls

---

*"I get scared to let my guard down
because of the fear of being hurt again."*

— *Unknown*

Walls are designed for multiple reasons. They are used to protect anything from entering, exiting, and containing whatever is inside. They are also used as a means of separation between spaces.

Our emptional walls are produced due to a lack of vulnerability and refusal or inability to be open, and we can't forget the safety and protection they provide. They are built over time, with no blueprint or plan, and construction commences from childhood at the first sign of disappointment or abandonment. The foundation is set with the first broken promise or failure to reciprocate or acknowledge or validate our feelings. And then, brick by brick, we build the walls for sustainable emotional safety that takes us far into adulthood.

I saw a quote that said, "you are not afraid of new love; you're afraid of old pain." The more I read it, the more I wanted to dig into it and understand that we are not afraid to fall in love and be loved by another soul, but we are terrified of reliving the pain that existed in our last relationship.

Only those who have been hurt repeatedly or on the deepest level will understand the notion of what I like to call soul hurt. It's deeper than a broken heart and goes far beyond betrayal. A soul hurt is a fracture to an emotional connection that is etched in your memory. Emotional pain has the ability to manifest physically. It's a different kind of ache and pain. Your heart physically hurts in ways you can't explain to another person or yourself for that matter, and it finds a way to filter into future relationships and friendships if it remains unhealed.

It's the kind of hurt where the building of a wall is inevitable and causes one to reinforce the walls of protection as means to ensure a soul hurt is never endured again. Why? Because when we are guarded, safety surrounds us, and the stronger and higher the walls, the safer we feel. If we need to choose between risking our safety versus being alone, many will choose the latter.

So let me ask you something that you can turn around and ask yourself. Are you a notorious gatekeeper of your heart? Do you have a wall around you constructed of bricks and mortar to avoid hurt? The answer is probably yes. My next question is, Why? Why do you have your guard up? Why do you deliberately build emotional walls? I ask because, for us to break down the walls brick by brick, we need to understand why they are there in the first place. We need to recognize the hurt before moving forward and removing the rest of that wall that keeps us from living, loving, and receiving love.

Let's stop blocking ourselves from living whole lives and receiving genuine love. I dare us to step out and understand that we are not emotional masonries. Let's dismantle our sacred walls and understand that there is an even greater reward on the other side despite the significant risk, and doing so will allow our souls to speak and breathe.

Be Inspired!

Privacy & Oversharing

"Privacy is a source of survival."

— *@theinspiredintrovert_*

We are the most connected generation with immediate access to anyone we want, anywhere globally. Yet, so many people suffer from an immense sense of loneliness that some find to be incurable.

There is this phenomenon with social media these days where people share everything down to what they eat in a day and wear in a week! So, number one, I ask why anyone should care? And number two, I wonder at what point did our lives become overexposed? I also wonder if we are using social media as a means to fill a void. I understand that there is the keeping informed factor which I believe is essential from a current affairs perspective. We use social media to transfer information that we rarely see on mainstream outlets, especially when it comes to social justice. I'm all for that, but I think we need to examine the other face of social media. Privacy and oversharing.

What do we lack in our lives that we value the opinion of a perfect stranger? Why do likes, follows, and subscribers hold so much weight on our self-worth? The desire for connection and engagement is so deep that people don't care where it comes or what they need to do to get it, as long as it fills the empty space.

We have deliberately put ourselves in fishbowls as we seek validation from outside sources, and I question what happened to us validating ourselves and having that form of self-love as enough? Could it be that where there is a lack of privacy, there resides a lack of authenticity?

Has someone ever told you that you are private? And not in a congratulatory manner but more accusatory as if there is something wrong with you? These days being private is an unfavourable trait, and I still can't figure out why it's negatively viewed.

When one lives life privately, people think it's due to lack of trust, being anti-social, past criticism, or fear of not being accepted. In my private yet humble opinion, privacy is a personal choice that is not up for debate.

I am so private; sometimes, I don't even know what's going on in my life; it's funny, but it's true. It's one of the many reasons I keep a journal, as it's the place I unearth the things I shelter in my head and heart. In full transparency, my privacy is deliberate. I share what I want, with whom I choose to share it. My privacy has nothing to do with lack of trust or being an introvert; it's how I choose to move through my life, and I'm happy here. Everyone else's job is not to understand why we are private. Their job is to respect our privacy.

Ok, so I can't have us going through this week without speaking about our relationships. Loving in private is one of the healthiest forms of protecting your relationship because there isn't any outside influence on how your relationship should or should not be going. It's just between you and your person. Perhaps loving in private is a way of throwing a safety net on our relationships to keep them and their contents secure. Here they can remain sacred, safe and maintain their authenticity.

You have a lot to ponder this week, so here are a few things I want you to consider. Let's normalize that dating in private, fighting in private and loving in private are all ok. Why? Because not everything needs to be seen, known or a conversation. Not everyone needs an all-access pass to what's happening or not happening in our lives.

Lastly, can we also normalize not putting a microscope on our lives and instead ask ourselves what is missing in us that we feel the need to share everything?

"Life must have its sacred moments
and its holy places. We need the infinite,
the limitless, the uttermost – all that can give
the heart a deep and strengthening peace."

– A . Powell Davies

Be Inspired!

Week Forty-five

Lost & Found

"Losing yourself in an attempt to keep someone else is one of the greatest abandonments of our time."

— *Vienna Pharaon*

The Oxford dictionary defines the word lost as the inability to find one's way, not knowing one's whereabouts. It describes the word found as having discovered something by chance or unexpectedly.

We know that everything that begins needs to end. I want to have memories of my interactions and relationships and remember the sight, taste, smell, and sound of them all, but I also want to look in the mirror and recognize my reflection. We must refrain from getting lost in our jobs, family or friend circles, or love relationships. I believe our goal should be to maintain our individuality by any means necessary, understanding that those committed to loving and appreciating us will meet us where we are.

Have you ever stared at your reflection and didn't know who was staring back at you? Have you ever forgotten what you are passionate about or couldn't have a conversation with yourself because you didn't know what to say?

The thing about losing yourself is that it looks different for everyone, so it's challenging to recognize the signs in a friend or loved one. When I think of what it looks like, I imagine it could be a loss of interest in something you once loved. It could be no longer knowing what you like or dislike. Music no longer stirs you like it used to. Laughter is a faint memory unless you are with certain people. You almost feel as if you are going through the motions and floating through life. You no longer have deep desires, and you can't recognize yourself.

There will eventually come a day where you become tired of feeling like a stranger to yourself, and you do the necessary mind, body and soul work required to become reacquainted. And one day, you look back with a crystal clear lens because hindsight truly is twenty-twenty. Sometimes we can be blind to everything that affects us negatively in hopes of salvaging the relationship we know needs discarding.

I wonder if any of you who are reading this have ever felt this way. I wonder if you have ever lost yourself in your career or your title. Maybe you lost yourself in a relationship you were only supposed to be a spectator to and not an active participant.

In full transparency, there was a time I wandered in the abyss of confusion and would spend hours waiting for something to come to me that I could write, and nothing would come to mind. I had lost my ability to write creatively and was unable to string a sentence together.

Then a year of clarity arrived, and not only did I find myself, but I recognized my reflection, and at that moment, words began to flow effortlessly and the more I saw myself, the more words came to mind.

The more people I talk to, the more I realize this type of lost and found happens often and typically takes place in the confines of our love relationships. We find ourselves consumed by the other person and fail to have that same level of a healthy obsession with ourselves. Slowly, the things that bring us a sense of fulfillment and joy disappear.

I had a conversation with someone about the dangers of losing ourselves and how easily it happens. We spoke about the importance of maintaining our individuality within our love relationships and how rare it is to find someone who encourages our personal growth and identity within the relationship while investing the time, space and energy to evolve as a couple.

For those who got lost along the way but through much determination, prayer, therapy, and self-discovery have found yourself; let's take a moment to bask in your dopeness and revel in the fact that when you thought it was the end, it was only the beginning.

For those who are still squinting at your reflection, trying to figure out who you are, what to say and what stirs you, keep it up because you will soon come to the point of enlightenment where everything becomes more evident. And as you find who you are, you will fall in love with yourself on a level that has never existed.

Losing yourself provides perspective.

Finding yourself supplies the strength to continue.

Gaining clarity allows you never to be lost again.

Be Inspired!

Vulnerability: Part One

---

*"Pride will always be the longest distance
between two people."*

— *Unknown*

Are you independent? If you can do it on your own, do you? Do you find it easier to depend on yourself because you can control any disappointment that may or may not come your way?

If you answered yes, join the club but don't get comfortable. I have learned that this type of thinking plays a significant role in the deterioration of our relationships. Instead, there needs to be a willingness to let our guard down and allow another person to come to our aid whether we feel we need it or not.

The more I pay attention to people and relationships, the more I notice that we have a knack for failing to show up and show out in our relationships. We tend to hold our feelings so close that no one ever knows what's on the inside except us, and what good is it there?

I understand we desire to avoid hurt and rejection, but we create a pressure cooker of emotions as we attempt to prevent this. We can choose between two results with a pressure cooker—either a slow, steady release or a messy explosion. It all depends on how we open it.

Often, we find ourselves tangled in the what-ifs of vulnerability and fail to allow ourselves the freedom of transparency. Yet, when we are transparent, we give ourselves the freedom to show up, and I am convinced that is the moment our relationships will begin to thrive.

Many of us have a tough time expressing how we feel, seeking help and asking for what we want and need, and I understand much of that stems from reoccurring disappointment and the ease of solely relying on ourselves. I understand the desire to guard our hearts to dodge bullets of hurt, manipulation, and so many other things that occasionally find a home in our relationships.

And maybe there isn't anything wrong with protecting ourselves, but what we use as a means of protection could eventually become a vessel of destruction.

When our relationships lack vulnerability, they lack trust and what good is a relationship without trust? When we fail to trust another person with our softer side, we also fail to show our authentic selves and allow them to be our safe place. When we shut down emotionally, we have to remember in that process; we are emotionally shutting out the one who is willing to lift our layers. Although it's never our intention to deliberately push our loved ones away, it is still the result.

I believe a lack of vulnerability is a form of self-sabotage and also relationship sabotage, so there is some work we need to do as individuals. How are we supposed to bask in the fullness of love and joy if we suffocate the relationship before it has time to bloom?

I want to encourage us to let the right people into our head and heart space. I want us to find the words and muster the courage to open gradually like a slow release versus a violent emotional explosion that will scare away everyone involved. I won't sugarcoat what you may experience when you go through the process. Your hands will be damp and clammy, the words will get caught in your throat, and when you do speak, your voice will shake, and you may even cry for no apparent reason. It will be an uncomfortable experience at first, but it gets easier with time and please know that it's worth it in the end.

"Vulnerability is the only bridge,
to build connection."

– Brené Brown

Be Inspired!

Week
Forty-seven

Vulnerability: Part Two

"Vulnerability is not winning or losing.
It's having the courage to show up
when you can't control the outcome."

— *Brené Brown*

There is a misconception that only men struggle with vulnerability, but I am here to say it's tough for everyone. If we were never on level ground before, men and women are equally struggling with the act of vulnerability.

And not only is vulnerability problematic on its own, once you add personality traits, family upbringing and past emotional hurt and trauma into the mix, we have also concocted a recipe for being emotionally mute.

As mentioned in last week's inspiration, we touched on the fact that vulnerability has two key components; Trust and honesty. We cannot reserve trust and honesty for other people solely, we need to extend it to ourselves. While it's impossible to keep a secret from ourselves, it's not impossible to be dishonest. I think we do it more than we would like to admit. And maybe that is where the proper recipe for vulnerability begins.

Let's start by understanding that vulnerability is part of the healing process, and we can't heal unless we are willing to admit we are hurting. We need to trust our thoughts and feelings before stepping outside of our realm to trust and be vulnerable with another soul.

You will recall I often say that not everyone needs to or should have access to you. Family ties are not equivalent to an all-access pass into your sacred space. And the reason for this is because I am a firm believer in the idea that before we open up, we need to ensure that our feelings are in a safe space. Even if the other person disagrees, they still take the time to hear us and acknowledge our feelings. I'm not sure if anyone realizes the power of having your feelings placed in safety. It's also one of the keys to vulnerability.

I think we need to be deliberate in our desire to be more vulnerable, and what I mean by this is that we trust the feelings that bubble to the surface of our souls rather than panic and push them down. We need to be uncomfortable and sit in our vulnerability.

Why? Because the task of being vulnerable means that we need to be emotionally available to the people we love. And when we hide parts of ourselves from our loved ones, it keeps us from fully living, trusting and loving.

Let's shift perspective and understand that vulnerability doesn't go one way. We also need to attempt to be a safe space for others who struggle with openness. Many of us naturally want to fix and take care of things and people, but I think we must learn and understand that we need to be receptive and silent most of the time. As much as we want to be heard, we also need to stop and embrace hearing.

Most of the time, when someone opens up and pours out to you, they don't want answers or suggestions. What they want is silence accompanied by understanding. That is why they chose you in the first place. It's a revelation I have come to embrace because I never realized how much I needed it until I sat in that space with someone. My safe space was a soft place to land. It was also a silent one, and it felt good because having a safe space for vulnerability is just as important as the act of being vulnerable.

I distinctly remember a time where I had to gather the courage to expose the softer side of myself to someone. When I tell you I was a wreck, I was an absolute wreck. I felt nauseated, barely slept, and food was not on the agenda. I knew what I wanted to say, but I was rendered emotionally mute. And it wasn't for lack of a safe space because, thankfully, that was created for me, but I wasn't trusting my feelings and had a brief moment of amnesia when it came to how I felt and that what I needed to say mattered.

But once I remembered who I was and pushed my anxiety to the side, I allowed my soul to say what she needed to say. And let me tell you, the release of allowing someone to see you in your emotional nakedness is a feeling I will never forget. And if you were to ask me to do it again, I know it would be easier, but I would still be hesitant because I am a work in progress. We are all a work in progress.

Remember that vulnerability is part of the healing process and doesn't happen overnight. For some of us, it's emotionally exhausting because it requires us to go to a place we rarely venture. But once we are there and our space is safe, we can move through the pain to a place of healing, one conversation at a time

*"Being vulnerable is the only way
to allow your heart to feel true pleasure."*

– Bob Marley

Be Inspired!

Week Forty-eight

The Purpose Of The Struggle

"Appreciate where you are in your journey,
even if it's not where you want to be.
Every season serves a purpose."

— *Unknown*

I used to get so annoyed when people would tell me, "what doesn't kill you makes you stronger, dear," And I wasn't sure if it was the statement or the "dear" at the end that enraged me more. Then I grasped the truth in those words, after near debilitating emotional cardiac arrest followed by the emotional jolt required to keep going. They were right all along!

If you have lived long enough, you will agree that pain and struggle are inevitable parts of some of our lives, and for those of you who haven't had to experience it, count it a blessing. Some of us will go through fire and come out with third-degree burns, others will sink into a valley so deep they have no idea how they will reach the safety of the level ground, and many will be in a dingy, drifting in the middle of the ocean with no paddle and no land in sight.

And although we understand the sometimes inevitable nature of the struggle, we don't have to like it, but perhaps we need to understand the purpose in the midst of it all because I believe there is one.

And yes, I know you're rolling your eyes, I am too, because I would much rather avoid past, present and future struggles and just go about life minding my business, staying hydrated and living happily ever after. Still, unfortunately, that's not how it works for all of us.

When we aren't in the frame of mind or have the capacity or emotional intelligence to learn from a situation, maybe we need to linger in it a bit longer. Perhaps it's a matter of unknowingly gaining the tools and insight within the trial to ensure we never end up in that situation again. I can honestly attest to that notion, hence why I am sharing.

I stayed in a five-year situation, five years too long! So yes, I squandered a good portion of my 30's with the wrong person, but I can say that I gained insight that positively changed my life's trajectory because of those hellish years. I learned about the qualities in a mate that are important to me, but most of all, I recognized what I deserve and what I don't deserve. I learned to not only hear my voice but recognize it and the power that dwells there. I learned that I am more than enough as I am. Is it just me, or do you feel like hi-fiving someone right now?

In all seriousness, I have realized that the purpose of the darkness is to appreciate the beauty of the light. And the state exists so we can embrace clarity. Sometimes we need to emerge from the fire to enjoy the rain's coolness, and once we understand the rain, the sunshine feels even better. I believe as we move through situations, there are lessons along the way. Each one prepares us for what rests on the other side.

"This too shall pass" is a phrase that we have probably all heard, and I know when we hear these things while we sit in the middle of the struggle, they infuriate us because we can't see further than the pain. I completely understand, but if you believe nothing else over the next few weeks, please believe that it does get better, and I am not saying it for the sake of filling a page. I am saying it because I am living proof.

Be Inspired!

*"The struggle is powerful.
The struggle is real, but even amidst suffering,
the struggle allows you to heal."*

– Taylor G. Peterson

Week Forty-nine

A Reason, Season Or Lifetime

---

*"Time does not dictate the level
of love or loyalty we receive."*

— *Unknown*

Have you ever stopped spending time with someone and realize you don't miss them? I suppose it's technically not supposed to feel good, but somehow it does.

I find that we sometimes think time and loyalty are synonymous, but they aren't. Perhaps we need to discover a new way to measure the quality of our friendships, love relationships and the company we keep and not let time be a significant deciding factor. Failure to do so sometimes causes us to remain in situations far longer than we need to.

Does the longer you stay at a job, show how much you like it? Does time indicate how much your boss likes you? Nope to both because time doesn't dictate anything except time, and knowing this, why would you stay in something just because you can add the years?

I overheard someone planning on ending their relationship. (As an aside, I am always in awe of people who have very private conversations in public spaces, but I digress) They said the reason was that being with their mate was more of a liability than an asset. They said there were too many issues and not enough benefits, and I nodded in agreement as if I knew this person, but they were on the right track. There is no sense in investing time, energy, love and affection in something that doesn't have a return in the long run.

I wonder if we need to look at our relationships as though they are a business of sorts. I know it's not the most romantic, but along with romance comes the necessity of logic and alignment. We not only need to be on the same page, but we also need to be moving in the same direction.

I'm not advocating moving from relationship to relationship, but I support being in healthy, stable and fulfilling relationships that are assets and not liabilities. I often wonder how people can go days and weeks without speaking to or having some communication with the person who has their heart. If we don't miss someone in their absence, perhaps that means their presence wasn't of much value. What are your thoughts on this? Do you have people in your life like this? Is this the state of your current relationship?

A quote states people come into our lives for a reason and season and a lifetime. The hopeful romantic in me likes to think that we all have a person out there who is all three. The reason they come into our life is to love us correctly. They remain with us through all of our emotional seasons, and they stick by our side for a lifetime.

We need to be more cautious of our time, how we spend it, and who we spend it with. The older I get I realize how precious my interactions with people are. I don't think we should feel obligated to entertain uneventful outings, shallow conversations and surface relationships. I'm not sure about you, but I want to make the best of my time and ensure I spend it with people investing in me as much as I am investing in them. Let's make memories and live fulfilled lives and do so with the right people.

Be Inspired!

Week Fifty

Understanding Our Needs vs Our Wants

---

*"Don't get so caught up in being independent
that you forget you NEED people…
Life is a team sport."*

— *@jquesmith*

A toxic narrative states we don't and shouldn't need another person, especially in our relationships. I believe the rationale behind this thinking is that it helps us maintain our independence, and while autonomy is good, we must remember that we are not an island. Humans are designed to be in communication and relationship with one another, and whether you want to believe it or not, we NEED one another.

I don't believe in depending on someone to the point of creating an unhealthy environment of co-dependency and the inability to decide on one's own. Still, I do believe in a healthy dependence and a healthy sense of need.

As I thought about the content for this week's dose of inspiration, I wanted to stress that we all lack in one area or another, and the reason is simple. None of us is perfect. We will always require things from our partners, and I consider those spaces to be healthy voids.

So when someone says I need you for whatever reason, I think that is a healthy void. You have created a space where your partner can be of assistance. If the void doesn't exist, there is no space for your partner and, therefore, no room for a partnership.

Suppose I enter into a relationship with the mentality that I don't need anything from anyone. What can I possibly expect this person to offer me, and therefore why would I expect them to stay?

We need to accept that the sense of need is ok in the confines of our relationships, and admitting that we lack something requires a level of self-awareness, emotional intelligence, and, you guessed it, vulnerability.

I came to this conclusion about some of the essential things I required in a mate, aside from the standard request of trustworthy, dependable, kind, and considerate. I said I wanted someone who could protect me both physically (if required) and emotionally. And someone who would create a safe space for my feelings and the softer parts of me. As an aside, I was only able to determine these things once I set aside my pride.

Then I thought about the word "want," and it's the desire to possess something. And I thought about the things above again, including my emotional protection, and concluded they aren't things I merely want. They are the things I need. Because to need is to require something essential.

I want someone handsome and bearded; I need someone who will provide a safe space for my emotions. I realize that our wants satisfy the surface, and our needs satisfy our hearts and souls.

I want you to think about your life and the relationships you have with people. Do you ever catch yourself thinking or saying you don't "need" anyone or anything? Do you find yourself wanting to be isolated and reside on the proverbial island? If so, I want you to be honest with yourself, identify where you have a void, dig up your vulnerability, and let that "someone" in your life know you need them to stand in the void and create a safe space for you.

May we all nurture the kind of love where we get what we know we want and everything we didn't think we needed.

Be Inspired!

Living Life On Purpose

---

*"Life would be a lot simpler
if we would just let it happen."*

— *Unknown*

Have you ever sat and thought about the fragility and shortness of life? And not in a morbid way but reflective? Think about how much time you spend planning compared to the time spent executing those plans. I find we plan so much that by the time the planning is complete, we don't have the energy to execute, and without execution, the plan is futile.

As I write this, I have been on this planet for 42 years and about 130 days. And if I am honest, I didn't begin to live life in my purpose until mid-2020. Yup, in the middle of a global pandemic, God decided it was time for me to re-evaluate where I was, why I was there and where He needed me to be.

We often go through the motions and live our lives within the parameters of how society and culture determine we should live. We aim for certain things by certain ages, and when we do not attain them, we consider it a failure or setback. But what if a perceived setback is the very thing we require to live in our purpose? What if every No received was slowly pushing us into alignment?

I am pretty sure if I had gotten the things I thought I wanted when I wanted them, I wouldn't be where I am today, doing what I enjoy. And maybe you can say the same thing. It's not to say we are in a rush, but we also have to stop setting tasks aside for a tomorrow that may never come.

Perhaps we need to promise ourselves to live in the moment alongside the anxiety and fear. Maybe we need to speak with honesty on things we like and don't like. And dare I say we tell people we love them, even if it means the love may not be reciprocated.

When the idea of this book came to mind, I set a plan and stood firm on a release date of January 2022. Then as I got to writing and re-writing, I was months ahead of schedule, yet I remained settled on my original release date. Why? Because I was afraid and wanted to delay putting myself out there as long as I could. So I recognized I needed to look at the why behind writing this book in the first place.

And after having a challenging conversation with myself, I adjusted amid the anxiety and fear I mentioned before and set 2021 as my official release because I can't live in my purpose if I keep putting it off for tomorrow. If I never experienced the trauma, I wouldn't have the words to write this book which I hope has given you insight as you move through your stuff. If I never had my heart mangled, there never would have been the opportunity for repair and space to love.

We don't need to have it all figured out, but we need an open mind and heart for the journey. We don't need to plan ourselves to death, but we need to perform the tasks required to live a whole life.

I have learned that life begins when we are open to receive what it has to offer. I challenge us to open up a little more every day and allow ourselves to live outside the parameters set up by our fear, anxiety, society and culture and do something that sets our souls on fire.

Be Inspired!

Soul Talks

"When used correctly, words are therapy and possess healing and freedom."

— *@theinspiredintrovert_*

Let's celebrate 52-Weeks of Inspiration! I hope you journaled yourself to a place of enlightenment and healing. I hope you asked yourself many tough questions and dug deep into the Why behind what you do and don't do, say and don't say. I hope you took the many opportunities to have conversations with your inner circles and loved ones to gain perspective and have a laugh and a cry together. Lastly, I hope you keep the conversations going.

I am curious to know if the fire from my soul was strong enough to start a spark in yours as you moved through these 52 weeks with me. Hopefully, it was.

This book writing process was challenging as I had to dig deep and not seek perfection but authenticity. It was surprising as well because I didn't know I had all of this inside me. At the end of it all, this was worth every finger cramp, every eye strain and associated migraine and every sleepless night. It was worth every moment.

I encourage you to share this book with a friend or have a book club and go through and reread it, journal again and discuss again. You will be amazed how your thought process changes over time. As I have said before, there is freedom in allowing our souls to open up and have Soul to Soul conversations.

I have a few questions for you before I let you go and live your enlightened lives.

1. Have your thoughts and behaviours changed in 52 weeks? How?

2. What stood out the most to you on this inspirational journey?

3. How will you continue to allow your soul to speak?

4. What week stood out to you the most and why?

I would love your feedback, so reach out to me on social media or via email and let's have a chat.

And last but definitely not least, THANK YOU! Thank you for telling your friends and family about **Soul Talks: 52-Weeks of Inspiration**. But most of all, Thank you for allowing me to be a part of your year.

Be Blessed, Be Healed & Be Inspired!

*"As soon as healing takes place,
go out and heal somebody else."*

– Maya Angelou

Acknowledgements

This book exists because God
decided to bless me with a curious mind,
the gift to write and the courage to ask many questions.
Thank you for the stillness
while I wrote my way to a place of healing.
Thank you for embedding a love
for the written word in every fragment of my being
and allowing me to rediscover creativity.

A Special Thank You to W.B.
You spoke life into this project without realizing it.
I appreciate you!

Thank you to my family and my inner circle for understanding
the importance of submerging myself in this collection.

About the Author

In this debut collection of writings, Talisha takes her inquisitive nature and love for the written word to a place she said she never thought would come to fruition. She looks at things from a critical and creative perspective, which led to her blog, The Inspired Introvert.

When asked who her literary favourite was, she had difficulty narrowing it down to just one. But beamed as Maya Angelou's name crossed her lips and said Maya Angelou made her not only fall in love with words but taught her to respect them.

Talisha does her best writing when she has no intentions of writing. This stress-free approach allowed her to create Soul Talks: 52-Weeks of Inspiration from a place of vulnerability and authenticity.

Talisha writes professionally for many businesses with services ranging from ghostwriting blogs, clarifying web content, personal bios and real estate listings. She prides herself in her versatility and knack for getting into her readers' heads and hearts.

Connect with her:
Instagram @theinspiredintrovert_ and @iamtalisham
Blog: www.talisham.wixsite.com/inspiredintrovert

CPSIA information can be obtained
at www.ICGtesting.com
Printed in the USA
BVHW081616271121
622656BV00003B/12